STUDY THE BIBLE

SIX EASY STEPS

November 2022

Gloria,

A great way to increase your relationship with God is to understand his word. Spend time to learn & increase your knowledge is the first thing. Hold in your heart his word & he will lead you in your christian walk.

Love,
Lorrie Salinas-Malins

Dennis C Stevenson Jr

www.dennis-stevenson.com

DEDICATION

To the small group at Christ Church who served as a guinea pig while I worked out this material. Thank you. Your grace and kind words were instrumental in convincing me that the material was worth sharing.

And to Scott, who shared the journey and read all the rough drafts.

Preface

IS THIS BOOK FOR YOU?

WOULD YOU LIKE TO FEEL CONFIDENT about what the Bible says? Would you like the comfort of knowing God's answers to challenges in your life? Would you like to join a Bible conversation at church and feel like you have something to say?

If you knew how to study the Bible, you could have all these things and more!

Think about being asked a question about the Bible and immediately knowing the answer. Consider the satisfaction of knowing what God has to say about a situation you are facing in your life. Imagine yourself saying something insightful about a Bible verse in your small group.

Many Christians believe a long list of barriers keeps them from studying the Bible and experiencing all these things. The real issue isn't what they think it is. **Most people don't know how to study their Bible because no one has shown them how!**

No one becomes a Christian and immediately knows how to study the Bible. Everyone needs to be shown how to do it. And the miracle of God's word is that anyone CAN do it!

- You don't have to go to Bible College or Seminary
- You don't have to know Greek or Hebrew
- You don't need to learn a long, complex process
- You don't have to be a genius

My name is Dennis Stevenson. I've been studying the Bible for more than twenty-five years but I didn't go to Bible School or Seminary nor did I have to learn Greek or Hebrew. I've converted this experience into a simple method that involves just six easy steps and no confusing terms.

I learned how to study the Bible because people showed me how it's done. Over the years, many godly men and women have invested in me. They worked with me to teach me the basic steps. Then they gave me books and resources that helped me refine my skills. I listened, I learned and most importantly I practiced.

If I can do it, so can you! This book will show you how.

I know what it's like to learn. I hate it when I'm taught things I don't need to know. I will not repeat that mistake with you. I've boiled down everything into the skills you really need to know to succeed.

In this book, I will show you the six easy steps that will turn you into an effective Bible student. We will go through them slowly and clearly. When I'm done, you'll probably think all I did was share some common sense. Divine common sense!

Before you are done with the last chapter you will actually study a short book of the Bible. I'll take you through every step with advice and guidance. I'll even share my own study notes with you so we can compare what we learned. But you will study the Bible for yourself.

When you are done, not only will you will have gained knowledge and confidence. You'll also have a set of study notes that will let you go back and review what you discovered. And you'll have the experience to do it again and again.

This book is definitely for you! All you need to do is start reading and commit until the end. I've done the hard work; you follow along. If you do this, the benefits I've described will be yours.

Foreword

PASTOR ADAM BAILIE

I love to study the Bible. That love has not always been a part of my life, though, and it hasn't even always been a part of my Christian life. In 1999, while in my university studies, I began attending a church under the leadership of a senior pastor who loved to study the Bible. His preaching demonstrated that love. He carefully unpacked what the particular text meant first to the original hearers and then how it applied all the way to the church today. I simply could not get enough. The Word was coming alive in every paragraph, and the implications to my life were gloriously transformative. As I became more enthralled with the living Word of God, that pastor began to train me, as someone had trained him, to study with precision, anticipation, and careful application. I have never been the same.

Though those days of discovery and awakening were many years ago now, their affect has not lessened in my life. Because the primary author of the Bible is the infinite God of heaven and earth, there is no end to the value and depth of the Scriptures. Nothing excites me more than seeing again, or for the first time, some worship inducing reality revealed from the mind and heart of God on the page of my Bible. That passion for God's Word gives me a special affection for those who share that passion and are seeking to instill it in other Christ followers today.

That's why I commend this practical tool from my friend and ministry colleague Dennis to you with joy and expectancy for God's work through it in your life. Dennis is equal parts precision and passion for the power of God's Word to impact you. He has pored over not just the theory of study, but the practical implementation that can best serve you as an eager disciple of Christ. He has taught, taught, and re-taught the content of this book. He has wept with joy to see it impact God's people as they've studied and discovered the Bible for themselves. He has prayed already for you, long before your eyes got to these words, that your life would be changed through your study of God's book to you, the Bible. So pray, read, dig, journal, and discuss this great resource. And above all let it drive you into God's presence and power through the study of His Word like never before!

"Do your best to present yourself to God as one approved, a worker who has no need to be ashamed, rightly handling the word of truth." (2 Timothy 2:15 ESV)

Adam Bailie
Lead Pastor - Christ Church - Gilbert, AZ

CONTENTS

Introduction

WHAT TO EXPECT IN THIS BOOK

THIS BOOK BEGAN IN THE LIVING ROOM of a friend's house. Ten of my friends had gathered for a small group Bible study and we were struggling. The study wasn't making sense and we didn't know what we were doing. Some people were quietly lost while others were full of questions. It wasn't going well.

The small group wasn't new and the people in it varied in terms of their experience as Christians. Some had been believers for a long time while others were relatively new in their faith. That didn't seem to matter. Most of the people were confused and were not getting a lot out of the study.

We finally decided to stop and spend time preparing ourselves to study the Bible. I created six lessons which laid out the basic steps of Bible study and the group soaked them up. Then we took a short book of the Bible and practiced what we had learned for another 4 weeks.

The results were shocking! As we resumed the Bible study, those people who had been lost began to connect what was happening and make contributions to our discussion. The people who had questions felt like they had a structure to help them understand. Everyone felt much more prepared and engaged.

This book will take you on that same journey of learning and discovery.

It doesn't matter if you are a new Christian or someone who has been a believer for 40 years. Odds are, you haven't been taught how to study the Bible. Many beloved saints have lived the majority of their lives without this basic skill.

You might think that you need to know Greek or Hebrew in order to study the Bible. You don't. You just need to be willing to follow a few steps and spend a little time. You'll be surprised at what you can learn from God's word with the background that you already have!

This book is designed to produce amazing results just like we saw in our small group. You can be the recipient of these benefits if you learn the simple principles I'll share.

The first part of the book is entitled "Getting Ready", and that's exactly what you'll be doing. I'll take you through the information you need to know in order to study the Bible. You'll probably be surprised at how much it sounds like common sense.

There are six chapters in the Getting Ready section, and they will cover all the tools you need to know.

Chapter 1: What is the Bible? sets the groundwork for the study by considering what the Bible is. You'll find many opinions if you ask around. We want to get to the bottom of the matter so that everything that follows is grounded in truth.

Chapter 2: Choosing the right kind of study looks at a wide range of different ways that you could study the Bible. You might be surprised at the diversity that falls under the heading "studying the Bible". You may even be doing one or more kinds of study today without even knowing it!

Chapter 3: Understanding the Big Picture and Chapter 4: Tools for Understanding look at the different tools that you will use in your Bible study. As I already said, you don't need to know Greek or Hebrew. The tools are simple and straight-forward. You've probably already been exposed to them. You just need be reminded.

Chapter 5: Applying what you learn will show you how to take your understanding of what the Bible says and accurately apply it to your life. Studying the Bible is about life transformation, not just new facts to master. Once you've learned this, you will have the ability to see what God is asking you to do – or commanding you to do.

Chapter 6: Using resources wisely will introduce you to a broad list of resources that you can use to enhance and support your study. Not only that, you'll understand when you should turn to study Bibles or commentaries and when you should use your own tools to uncover God's message to you.

Throughout these chapters, I'll explain what you need to know, but I'm also going to ask you to think about a number of thought-provoking questions. I'll give you space to write down your answers. The more you engage, the more you'll understand and the better you'll become at studying on your own.

In the second part of the book, "Using What You've Learned", we'll put all the study tools to use. Together we will study the book of Titus in the New Testament. The book of Titus is a short letter from the Apostle Paul to his friend and fellow pastor Titus. Paul has some clear points to make to Titus, and you will be able to apply those truths to your own life.

Chapter 7: A survey of Titus will introduce you to the book of Titus, its author, and audience. Following the study steps, you'll spend much of this first study lesson getting oriented to the structure of the book and how Paul uses it to communicate

Chapters 8-10: Studying Titus will dive into the three chapters of Titus roughly one chapter per lesson. This is where we'll dig into the text and discover what it has to say.

Chapter 11: What Next? will summarize what you've learned and will offer some practical encouragement for what you might consider next.

During the Bible study portion of the process, this book will become your workbook. I've included the questions to answer and I give you space to write down your answers. If you simply follow my lead, you'll find that it's simple to work your way through the text of Titus. I'll even share my answers so you can compare and find new ways to hone your skill.

Everything you'll learn in this book is a template you can use on your own. With a little practice, you'll become proficient at following the six-step process to reading and understanding what the Bible has to say, and then applying it to your own life.

You can read this book and do the study by yourself. That would be very rewarding. However, if you want a deeper impact, consider doing it with a friend. Just like my small group went through this together over 10 weeks, you could meet weekly with a friend to discuss each chapter. If you did one chapter per week, you'd be done in less than three months.

Who do you know that would benefit from knowing this? They don't have to be an expert. You can learn together. Write down a name and give them a call. They will probably be glad you thought of them!

I would like to do this study with: _____

Maybe a name will come to you later. That's fine. It's never too late to invite someone to study the Bible with you! Just stay open to the possibility of teaming up.

If you don't have a friend to do this with, don't worry, it's not a requirement. What really matters is what you learn and how you will grow spiritually as a result of reading.

This book is designed to be your workbook. It has blanks and spaces to write in your answers. If you don't like writing in your books, that's fine, I've published a FREE Study Guide with all the same questions and answers you can download and use instead. Get your Study Guide on my website at:

https://www.dennis-stevenson.com/StudyGuide

Let's get started!

Part One

GETTING STARTED

Chapter One

WHAT IS THE BIBLE?

ONGRATULATIONS FOR DECIDING TO LEARN how to study the Bible! In the pages that follow, I'll provide you with the information you need to know in order start studying for yourself. In this chapter, I want to focus on understanding what the Bible is.

You've obviously decided to start studying the Bible for some reason. It might be to better understand your pastor or to finally learn what the Bible has to say, or perhaps because you want to join a Bible study group and don't want to look like a beginner.

Believe it or not, the Bible itself gives us reasons to study it. When we properly understand what the Bible is and what it has to say to us, we find even more reasons to open it up and start to study it.

That's what I want to do in this first chapter. I want to show you what the Bible is and what it truly has to say. I believe this will give you even more motivation to study the Bible. I also think it will raise your expectation for what you will gain when you study the Bible.

The Bible is God's message to us. In its pages, God introduces Himself to the reader and displays His holiness and sovereignty. At the same time we see ourselves as infected with sin and hopelessly cut off from God. This paints a terrible picture for us, cut off from God and responsible for the consequences of our sin. Fortunately, the Bible doesn't stop there. The continuing narrative arc of the Bible is how God reaches out to us and makes a way for us back to Him through Jesus' sinless life and payment of our sin-debt. This is God's message and He wants us to know what He has to say.

The Bible, however, is not a general message communicating broad concepts in non-specific language. Quite the opposite is true. The Bible is very specific in what it says, and this matters a lot!

The Bible is the Word of God

Throughout both the Old and New Testaments, the writers of the Bible refer back to it as "the word of God". That is to say, the very words that God wanted to communicate to us.

Look up the verses below and briefly write down what they say about the word of God.

Psalm 119:11 _____

_____

Psalm 119:105 _____

_____

Proverbs 30:5 _____

_____

John 6:67-69 _____

_____

Hebrews 4:12 _____

_____

This dramatically changes how we think about the Bible. It's not talking in concepts or just telling stories with a moral (although at various times it does do those things as well). It uses very specific words, and these words matter.

The theme of Psalm 119 is God's Word. To the psalmist, this was the five books of Moses where God declared his covenant with Israel and passed down His law. In verse 11 the writer says that he has memorized God's words so that he would not violate them and stand guilty before God.

Continuing on in the same chapter, the psalmist says that God's Word illuminates his path. It makes his path clear so that he knows what to do. This is similar to verse 11 because the context is about living a life pleasing to God by obeying His law.

Proverbs 30 says that God's word is pure and untainted, and therefore true. Because of this, it protects those who rely upon it because what it says is dependable and reliable.

When Jesus asked the disciples if they wanted to leave Him and follow someone else, Peter objected. He recognized that the very words Jesus spoke were different than the words that he heard from everyone else. Jesus words were the only means he had of accessing eternal life.

In Hebrews, we see the word of God is unique and has unparalleled power in our lives. God's words have the ability to get into the secret parts of our lives and see the truth that might not be visible from the outside. Because of this, when God judges us, He judges the complete person, not just the outside actions.

In these passages, we see that God is serious about His word. It has power and the ability to change our lives: saving us, keeping us obedient, giving us life, showing us what to do and judging us.

In everyday conversation, we use words to communicate with each other. God chose the same communication style and expressed Himself in words which we have today as the Bible. Those words were written down in the form you can buy today at any Christian bookstore, or read on the internet.

We should take God's word very seriously. The Bible makes it very clear that God's word is capable of far more than we can accomplish ourselves. It does the work that only God can do.

Since the Bible is communication from God, I want to make a point about communication. It's something that will come up again later in this study. But it's really important and I want to get it out early so we don't have any confusion.

The purpose of communication is to pass a specific message from a speaker or writer to a listener or reader. The speaker determines what the message is, and the purpose of communication is to see the message accurately delivered to the person who is listening. Any break-down in this process has a very specific definition: *miscommunication.*

Perhaps you've played the game "grapevine" before. It goes by a lot of different names, but the concept is very similar. One person in a group whispers a message into the ear of the next person. This message is passed from person to person until everyone in the group has heard it and passed it on. Finally, the last person and the first person share their version of the message. Often, the two messages are unrecognizable. Everyone gets a great laugh trying to sort how the message got so messed up.

With the Bible, God is the speaker and we are the listeners. God has a specific message that He intends to communicate. Our role is to receive that message exactly how He intended it. We don't get to put words in His mouth. We don't get to add our own little flair or opinions to His message.

In the game of "grapevine", that kind of miscommunication is funny. But when we are dealing with God's word, we don't want any miscommunication. Just like Peter said, if we miss out on what God has to say, we are missing out on the words of life. When miscommunication happens, bad things generally follow.

The Bible is communication from God, and we want to know *exactly* what He has to say. If we make it say what we want to hear, it ceases to be God's communication and it loses all of its power and value.

God is the Author of the Bible

Our modern Bible is a collection of many different writings. It was written by at least 39 different people who wrote different portions over a 1,500 year period of time. Despite the number of human writers, we believe that God is the actual author.

The Bible gives us a logical argument for a single author. From beginning to end, the Bible has a consistent message. It describes God in unwavering terms. It presents our human condition with different words, but a common assessment of what we need.

Throughout the Bible, we see the progressive unveiling of a unified story. God the Creator makes man, who sins and is separated from God with no ability to return. What follows is the dramatic revelation of God's plan to redeem the people who rejected Him. It's not done in one grand movement, but in a series of steps that proceed to the revelation of Jesus and His sinless sacrifice.

The consistency and coherent plot line of the Bible point to a single author who is assembling the storyline carefully with a plan for what needs to be said. There is no reasonable way that so many people could have made all the parts of our Bible hang together so well.

It's not just logic that points us to an understanding of God as the author. Several of the individual men who wrote portions of the Bible said that God was the author who brought it all together.

Read the following verses and jot down a couple things you observe about who they say wrote the Bible.

2 Peter 1:21 _____

_____

2 Timothy 3:16 _____

_____

Peter, one of Jesus' closest disciples, was writing a letter to fellow believers. In this part of the letter, he said that his readers have even more evidence than prior generations, and they ought to pay attention to it. The word of God had been communicated and confirmed to them and was not a matter of anyone's opinion.

Peter is very clear that the Holy Spirit "carried along" the human writers to express what God wanted to have written. This language says that while the human writers used their own style of writing, what they communicated was exactly what God wanted us to know.

Paul, the great missionary apostle, gets even more personal with what he says. In writing to his protégé Timothy, he says that the Scriptures were "breathed out" by God. That's what the word "inspired" means.

According to what Paul wrote to Timothy, the very words of the Scriptures were carried on God's breath. There were not the ideas of the men who actually wrote them down.

However, those men did write them down, and they have been preserved for us to read today. Undoubtedly part of the history of some of the Bible was communicated from person to person via oral tradition, but at some point, it was written down in manuscripts and copied over and over again until it came to us today. God superintended this transmission to ensure that the message He communicated did not get corrupted like in the game of "grapevine."

The Bible is Inerrant

Inerrant is something of an old-fashioned word these days. It has a very simple meaning, though. It means "without error". When we say that the Bible is inerrant we are describing a quality that it possesses apart from every other book that has been written.

Since God is the author, what He says expresses His character. If God had the character of a human, we would expect the Bible to be slightly incomplete, riddled with errors and off point occasionally. People don't know everything and make mistakes. If God had the character of a trickster, we'd expect the Bible to have misleading sections and other parts that were wrong just to mess with us.

God's character is holy, true and omniscient. He knows everything, so we don't need to worry that there are things He doesn't understand. He is holy, which means that He is without sin or lying. Finally, He is true, so what He says is also true.

As we consider the Bible, we do well to also remember that God is omnipotent. That is, He can do anything. This means that even though the writers were human, and lived in an age when they understood less of the world than we do today, what they wrote remains true for us. God's power is responsible for that. He ensured that the individual writers did not stray into errors as they expressed the message He wanted them to convey.

God is also eternal and unchanging. This is quite different from you and me. We are both finite and changing. Our opinions and beliefs grow and change as we age and encounter different experiences. Not so with God. His perspective on events 2,000 years ago is exactly the same as His perspective today. So even though the Bible was originally penned long ago, its truth is still true today.

All of these ideas are wrapped up in the meaning of "inerrant". Because of who God is, His word was true when it was first written and is still true for us today. Even though it was written by imperfect humans with ancient worldviews, God ensured that what they wrote was true and is applicable to us today.

Just because we say that the Bible is inerrant doesn't make all the hard or confusing sections suddenly easy. Some parts still challenge brilliant and skilled Bible students. But through it all, we have confidence and faith in the Author of the Bible. There is neither reason nor cause to doubt what He says, even as we work, or even struggle, to understand it.

In the Bible, we see God's message to us perfectly preserved, just as He intended it. It is a message for all ages and times, just as He is the God of all ages and times. Since God isn't confused or uncertain, His message is exactly what He wants it to be. Our job is to engage, study and understand.

All of the Bible is the word of God and is inerrant. We say "The Bible IS the word of God." It does not contain the word of God.

Containing the word of God implies that some of what it contains is not the word of God. If that were the case, we would have to question everything in the Bible and ask "Is this part of God's message?" The result would be nothing but uncertainty and doubt.

The same God who inspired the writers to communicate His message also prevented those writers from adding in their own thoughts and opinions. It would be silly of us to assume that God could give the writers His message and ensure that it was communicated perfectly how He wanted, but then couldn't stop them from writing more than what He wanted. Since God wanted to communicate with us, we believe that the Bible is exactly and only what He wanted to say.

We don't get to pick and choose the parts we want to believe or study. All of the Bible is the word of God and is suitable for us to engage. That doesn't mean that it's all equally relevant to every situation we face, but it can all be used to reveal God, point out our sin problem and show us God's plan of redemption.

The Bible is our Final Authority

The three truths we've already looked at lead to this final point. Because the Bible is God's message to us and because it says exactly what God wants it to say and because it is without error, the Bible communicates with authority.

In the Bible, we see God as He reveals Himself. He is telling us exactly what we need to know to see Him correctly. The Bible is the full revelation of God. When it comes to understanding God, His character, His attributes or His standard, there is no other source. No one knows God better than He knows Himself. He is the best qualified to reveal Himself.

So as you think about God, it's tempting to fill in the blanks with what you've read in other books, or what you've heard from friends, or even what you want to be true. That would be ignoring the authority of the Bible. The best approach to getting to know God is to study what He has already told you about Himself.

In the Bible, we also see ourselves exactly as God sees us. When we evaluate ourselves or each other, it's very difficult to pick a measuring stick to compare ourselves against. We are entirely subjective. But God has communicated His standards to us. He points out our sin and our separation from Him.

Granted, this isn't exactly happy news that we like to dwell on. But as we've already established, it's true. It is something that we all need to deal with if we want to have any kind of a relationship with God.

In the Bible, we see God in action to redeem us and bring us back into relationship with Him. This is the great news that follows the bad news. We don't have to fix ourselves. God's plan provides a way for us to come to Him, just as we are.

The Bible shows us what it looks like to have faith. It begins with faith that God has actually provided a way. But it goes far beyond that into the kind of faith that trusts in God's provision of a savior. This kind of faith in something we can't see or touch is unnatural. We benefit tremendously by seeing it modeled and having it explained in the Bible.

If you ever think that you've got a great idea for making God happy or for pleasing God, check the Bible. Your idea has no authority on its own. It only has merit or value to the degree that it aligns with what God has already done – and told us about.

Finally, the Bible explains to us how we should live lives that please God. There are lots of ideas floating around today telling us how to live "the good life". All other ways of living that don't follow the pattern outlined in the Bible are guaranteed to fail us and will not result in a "Well done, good and faithful servant" when we see Jesus face to face.

Because the Bible is the word of God, it is the final authority for how we know who God is, how we understand our relationship with God and what we need to do about that. As you are faced with decisions, the Bible is a great place to turn to for advice and wisdom on how to proceed. Studying the Bible is how you will know what it says.

Remember at the beginning of this chapter, I said that the Bible gives us its own reason to study? This is it. Take whatever reason motivated you to buy this book and add to it that only the Bible is

God's message to us about who He is, who we are, His plan of salvation and how we should live to please Him. Together these are all great reasons to study the Bible.

Living what you've learned

Now that you've read this chapter and gotten to learn a little bit about the Bible, how does this impact how you live? It's one thing to gain some knowledge but quite another thing to let that knowledge change you.

Take a moment and reflect on the questions below. Given what you've learned about the uniqueness and authority of the Bible how would you answer today? Do you think that's a good answer, or would you like to see change and growth in your life so that you could answer differently?

How often do you read the Bible? _____

_____

_____

Do you understand what it says; are you striving to go deeper? _____

_____

_____

In what areas of your life do you need to begin to obey what you read in the Bible? _____

_____

_____

Chapter Two

CHOOSING THE RIGHT STUDY

WHEN YOU THINK ABOUT STUDYING THE BIBLE, does a specific picture of what that looks like spring into your mind? Do you imagine a desk covered in books and notes and a well-worn Bible? Perhaps you think of a computer with lots of documents and study resources open. These could all be accurate images, but they tend toward one specific type of Bible study.

The majority of this book will be diving into a specific type of Bible study called "Textual Bible Study". That's not the only kind of study that's available. Options range from simple with minimal time commitment to in-depth and lots of time required. You might already be using one of these study methods and not even know it!

In this chapter, I'll share six different types of Bible study. Together we'll consider how those methods work and what kinds of objectives they satisfy. Not all methods are intended to accomplish the same goals. By the end of the chapter, you'll be able to identify which types of study work best for you right now, and put together a plan to make the most of your study time.

Not all types of study are created equal. Not all types of study are appropriate for every situation. As you consider your own study objectives, picking the right study is a critical first step.

Before we look at the different methods of studying the Bible, it's important to understand the Biblical principle of maturity and how it relates to studying the Bible. This will lay a helpful framework for you to understand how the different methods might work together.

Principles of Study Selection

The Bible lays out a very clear picture of the process that we go through as believers. The spiritual word is "sanctification", but we might think of it as "growing up". The picture of growing up spiritually is quite useful to help us grasp a couple key points.

We should all be familiar with the idea of growing up. We all grew up from children to where we are today. You may also have children of your own, and have watched them grow from babies. Even if you don't have kids, you probably know someone who does have kids and you've been able to watch the process from a distance.

The key concept of growing up is transitioning from being able to do a little to be able to do more. Initially, babies communicate through crying and other inarticulate sounds, then they progress to a few words, then simple sentences. Children build on simple sentences until they can communicate complex ideas. As adults, we are able to communicate abstract ideas, and even read books like this.

The same idea applies to our faith and Christian life. We begin capable of a little bit, and over time with work, we are able to do more and more. The writer to the Hebrews expresses this with a food metaphor in Hebrews 5:12-14. Grab a Bible and read those verses then consider the questions below.

What expectation does the writer have for his audience? (Verse 12):

_____

_____

What is the real circumstance lived out by the audience? (Verse 12):

_____

How does the writer describe spiritual milk? (Verse 13) _____

_____

_____

How does the writer describe spiritual meat? (Verse 14) _____

_____

_____

This isn't the only time that the metaphor of meat and milk is used in the Bible. Paul uses it in a similar way in 1 Corinthians 3:2-3. Look that passage up and read through it. It will only take a couple moments.

Just as babies are only capable of drinking milk, we see that metaphor used to describe people who are spiritual babies. There's nothing wrong with spiritual babyhood. Just as with people, we all start out as a baby. It's a normal part of the process of growing up.

However, both Paul and the writer to the Hebrews are expressing disappointment and concern that their readers are *still* spiritual babies. By now they should have grown up and moved beyond baby food. It's the same kind of thing we might think if we saw a teenager who was still drinking milk out of a bottle. We'd say "that's not right!"

The goal of spiritual growth is to be able to handle spiritual meat. Meat is very different from milk. It requires strong muscles and teeth to chew, and a strong stomach to be able to digest. You and I probably don't think twice about eating a good steak. Our bodies and muscles have developed to be able to handle that.

This principle of milk and meat is very useful to help us understand different kinds of Bible studies. Just as babies need milk, some Bible studies are appropriate for those who are still spiritual babies. They are simple enough that the student doesn't need much skill or experience, and they teach lessons that are appropriate to a simple understanding of the faith and obedience.

Other studies are more like meat and are rightfully intended for those who are more mature. These studies deal with more complex and difficult topics and rely upon a degree of spiritual maturity to be received correctly. If given to a spiritual baby, they would not achieve their appropriate outcomes.

Now that you are thinking about this spectrum of milk to meat, I want to remind you of something really important. Just because one type of study is simpler than what you are capable of digesting doesn't mean it has no use for you. Adults can still drink milk and eat soft foods. They aren't only for babies. In the same way, you can find great benefit in some of the more milk-like Bible study methods.

In many cases, the best way to grow is actually a balanced diet of both milk (simple) and meat (more complex) Bible study. As you read through the types that follow, think about each type of study and whether it would be a beneficial part of your balanced spiritual diet.

Study Method 1: Read the Bible

I know this sounds really obvious, but reading your Bible is a simple form of study. Reading promotes understanding and an awareness of the information that God chose to communicate in the Bible. In terms of the things that you can do on your own, this is probably the simplest.

As a study method, reading your Bible doesn't take you very deep into the meanings and what God has to say. It allows you to skim over the surface. To use another analogy, it's like snorkeling as opposed to scuba diving. You're always close to the surface.

The good news for Bible readers is that there are plenty of lessons on the surface that you can pick up. It doesn't take a really deep dive to find value when reading God's word. This is often why new believers or people seeking God are encouraged to read the book of John. The story is obvious, the truth is readily apparent and it doesn't take any special skill to discover what the message is.

If you want to read your Bible, believe it or not, you already have a secret weapon. His name is the Holy Spirit. He is a gift you received the moment you put your faith in Jesus. You received the Holy Spirit to live in you and walk with you. He helps you understand spiritual matters and intercedes for you with God. Even when you feel off or out of touch, the Holy Spirit is working on your behalf.

There are many different ways that you can read the Bible. Most of them relate to dividing it up into sections and reading through it over the course of a set period of time. A very common form of this is the annual reading plan.

If you want to read the Bible over the course of one year there are a number of different methods that you can choose from:

- Read straight through from Genesis to Revelation
- Read the books in the sequence they were written - this helps with some of the historical sections where you can get a better flow of events
- Read some of the Old Testament and some of the New Testament every day
- Read through the New Testament in a year or through the New Testament plus Psalms and Proverbs
- You can divide it up many different ways, including some plans that read some (shorter) sections multiple times and other sections (longer) only once.

If you search online for *Bible Reading Plans*, you'll get a huge number of options that you can pick from. Don't let the task sound too intimidating. It only takes about seventy-two hours to read the entire Bible out loud. That averages out to about twelve minutes per day if you did it every day for a year.

Other reading options that don't involve reading the whole Bible are plans that read through the book of Proverbs, one chapter per day each month by reading the chapter that matches the calendar day or one Psalm per day. These are all good methods to start engaging with the Bible.

In today's modern society, you don't even need to read the Bible for yourself. There are plenty of audio versions of the Bible available. You can listen to it in your car or while you walk. Granted, if you're doing other things while listening, you won't have your undivided attention on God's word, so you're likely to get less out of it, but this is still a great method to surround yourself with what God has said.

Study Method 2: Memorize the Bible

In our lives, we memorize all sorts of things. Birthdates, phone numbers, lines from movies we like, songs we hear on the radio. Why not memorize the word of God too?

In Psalms 119:11, David writes that he memorized God's words so that he would know what God wants from him and he could avoid sinning. This is a great use of the skill of memorization. Think back to Chapter One and all the reasons why we should study the Bible. If it's worth studying, it's probably worth memorizing as well.

Memorizing the Bible is more like milk than meat on our maturity scale. Just because a passage in the Bible has been committed to memory, we don't automatically know all the points that God is trying to make. But we do certainly get a good sense of the message that He is delivering.

David wrote that memorizing God's word helped keep him from sinning. When we memorize God's word, it becomes immediately accessible to us. We don't have to run to our Bible to look it up to see what God has to say to us. We don't have to rely on a friend or pastor to tell us what God has to say. It's right there in our own mind and heart.

Because God's word is the authority and is the truth, it's great to have it when you need it. This can be a real lifesaver:

- When you are tempted to do something wrong and need encouragement to make the choice that God would approve
- When you are down and need encouragement. The Bible calls Jesus the "Friend who sticks closer than a brother." If you can remember that you are not alone, it's a great encouragement.
- When you need to be reminded of your new identity in Christ. When you're struggling in your life, it's good to be

reminded that your sins are forgiven, you have direct access to God, the Holy Spirit lives within you and that you are a co-heir with Jesus.

- When you want to know the right thing to do. The Bible has many practical sections about how to live in a way that pleases God. By memorizing them, you can have them on the tip of your tongue for when you need to be reminded what to do.

Many people are intimidated by the thought of memorizing the Bible. "I'm not good at memorizing things," is a common excuse that is given.

I'm not here to argue with you about how skilled you are at memorizing. I do know that everyone is capable of memorizing something. We do it all the time as a part of our lives. We just end up memorizing mostly accidental things.

Memorization as a form of Bible study changes this dynamic. Instead of things with no eternal value, it focuses on memorizing the words that God has communicated to us. It's really no different than what we already do every day.

The other secret about memorization is that once you start, it becomes easier. Memorization is like a muscle. If you don't use it purposefully and regularly, it will be weak and not very helpful. However, if you take the time to use it, it will become fit and strong.

Bible memorization can be very similar to reading God's word. If you use it to fill in the unused minutes in your life it serves to keep your attention focused vertically. When you do that, your life will be changed.

If you would like to add Bible memorization to your study program, that's fantastic! Search online for *Bible Memorization Plan* and you'll find links to a long list of programs you can use. These plans will range from easy ones for beginners to more comprehensive ones for people with developed memorization skills.

An even better way to go with Bible memorization is to work with a friend. This provides invaluable encouragement and accountability.

It also gives you someone to practice with as you demonstrate your newfound knowledge.

Study Method 3: Meditate on the Bible

Biblical meditation consists of filling your mind with God's Word. It is completely the opposite of many modern ideas of meditation. When I talk about Biblical meditation, many people are forced to completely redefine their expectations.

Eastern meditation is a completely different practice which has absolutely nothing to do with Biblical meditation – despite the fact that both terms use the word "meditation". The objective of eastern meditation is to empty oneself of all thought, and thereby find transcendence or unity with the universe. This practice has no Biblical foundation or truth.

The Bible actually has a fair amount to say about meditation. Before reading any further, look at these Scriptures and write down what they have to say about meditation. These Scriptures provide both an Old Testament and a New Testament perspective on meditation – and if you look closely you'll see that they are very similar

Joshua 1:8 _____

_____

Philippians 4:8 _____

_____

In Joshua chapter one, God spoke to Joshua right after he was selected to succeed Moses. This is what God wanted him to know as he took up the mantle of leadership over the people of Israel. Joshua was to be obsessed with God. He was to think about God and God's word all the time. That's what the phrase "day and night" means. This is a great picture of meditation.

The first thing to note is that this command to meditate had an *object*. It was about something: namely the Book of the Law. This was the entirety of the word of God revealed at that time. God had revealed it to Moses, who in turn communicated it to the people. In it, God outlined what His commitment to the people looked like and what He expected of them in return.

The second thing to note is that the command to meditate had a *purpose*. God told Joshua he was to be careful to do everything that was written in the Book of the Law. In other words, God didn't want Joshua to mess up and do things wrong, or forget things.

Finally, we see that the command to meditate had a *method*. When God said "day and night", he meant "all the time." He wanted Joshua to continually be thinking about what God had said.

The Philippians passage is very similar. It doesn't directly use the word "meditate", but we can easily see the similarities. Paul was encouraging the church at Philippi to consume their thoughts with things that glorify and please God. Paul clearly doesn't want idle minds or empty minds. He wants minds which are filled with thoughts of God.

This, is Biblical meditation: filling your mind with God and His word.

As a form of study, Meditation works very well with both of the previous study methods we've considered. As you read the Bible, you will come across bits that stand out and grab your attention. Spend the rest of the day thinking about that little bit of God's word. Fill your mind with God's words. Memorization is a very close cousin to meditation because it already occupies a big space in our mind as we rehearse and commit to memory.

As you fill your mind with God's word, it will become familiar to you. You will start to gain a new perspective on what God has to say. You will be able to rehearse the commands and promises over and over. You can lose yourself in the truth that God has revealed about Himself and about you.

Rather than distancing ourselves from God's word, Biblical meditation brings God's word close until it becomes like an old friend. As you rehearse and repeat those words, considering them and contemplating what God is communicating with you, your life can't help but be impacted. The way you look at decisions will be through the lens of God's word and the values that you live out will be continually refreshed by what God has to say.

To be clear, Biblical meditation is more contemplative than analytical. Do you understand what God is saying in the passage? Have you considered the actual words He chose to use, and how they are shaping the message compared to other words that could have been chosen? Is there a command or a truth or a warning that He is trying to pass to you? Does God reveal an aspect of Himself that you can consider? Do you see the truth about yourself before God?

All of these are good questions to explore as you meditate on God's word. It doesn't take tools beyond a willing mind and a commitment not to be distracted while you consider.

Biblical meditation goes a little deeper than reading or memorization alone. In this, I think it's less milk-like and more like meat along the scale. As I've already said, it works well in combination with the other two. In fact, Biblical meditation is a wonderful compliment to all of the study options we will consider in this chapter.

Biblical meditation may not be the best technique for all passages. It works well for Scripture that is visually oriented, or where the passage has a very clear message. If you think a passage is complicated or tricky, you might avoid meditation and focus on the next study method instead.

Study Method 4: Textual Study

Most people naturally think of this study method when they hear "Study the Bible". Textual study is the process for understanding the message that God intended when He communicated the Bible to us. This study method focuses first on what God's word says to people generally and to you or I specifically so that we can properly live it out in our lives.

The textual method focuses on the words of the text to understand the message that is being communicated. It also looks at the way that ideas are structured and communicated to more fully understand the meaning that they contain. Based on this understanding of the message, an application for the student's life is developed and action is taken.

Much of the rest of this book will be diving into this study method, so I won't go into a lot of detail here. But I do want to point out the critical features so you can see how it fits in the overall list of study methods.

Textual study is critical for the "right handling of the word of God." In 2 Timothy 2:15, Paul instructs Timothy to study or to be diligent and put in the effort necessary so that he can properly handle (teach, obey, instruct others) the word of God.

Paul is making reference to the idea that Timothy would need to put in some effort to make sure that he had a correct understanding of what God's word had to say. If he didn't put in that work, he would not come to the right understanding of God and would not be able to teach effectively.

You don't have to be a pastor or a Bible teacher to be concerned with rightly handling the word of God. If you want to know what God has to say, then right handling is important for you. You also have influence in the lives of others and can use the truth of God's word to provide godly wisdom:

- When friends come to you for advice
- When you are working together with co-workers or on a team
- With family members in the normal course of interaction

This isn't a special skill that's reserved for the elite few. In 2 Timothy 2:2, Paul challenges Timothy to teach faithful men, who would, in turn, be able to teach others. Paul doesn't want Timothy, the pastor, to hoard this skill or knowledge. He wants it to be shared broadly and accurately.

This is the plan God has in place for us today. He wants us to engage with His word and understand what he has to say to us so that we can pass that on to others.

Doing a textual study method isn't just an exercise in knowledge acquisition. Learning and understanding is only the first step in the method. Typically a textual study follows this pattern:

1. Understand what the text means (from the author to the original audience)
2. Identify how it applies to me (either generally or specifically)
3. Determine what I must do because of the text.

This journey from discovery to action is the purpose of the study. Too often, the method ends after the first step and results in simply understanding. This is not an effective use of the method. Head knowledge does not result in life transformation. Only when all three steps in the pattern are followed does the study achieve its full and intended potential.

Textual studies can become very technical – but do not need to go that far. Even though this is the same kind of study that seminary professors teach young pastors, it's also a kind of study that can be approached by an everyday Christian.

As you will see, the textual study method is the beginning of the "meat" type of study. It also forms the foundation of the remaining two types of study we will look at. Both of these studies build off of the tools and techniques of textual study to make deeper studies with a different focus.

Study Method 5: Topical Study

The topical study method is similar to a textual study in many ways. It employs many of the same tools to understand what a passage says. The topical study is primarily interested in understanding what entirety of God's word has to say. Instead of focusing on one specific passage, the topical study picks a word or a topic and considers it throughout the full range of Scripture.

This approach considers all the references to the topic and identifies what Scripture teaches in each passage. By assembling all the teachings of the Bible on a given topic, the student is able to gain a well-rounded perspective that may be greater than what any one author needed to say to his audience.

Some common topics might include:

- Love
- Grace
- Forgiveness

By studying these topics you would be able to see all the different ways that the topic is addressed or handled throughout the Bible. By piecing these together you could understand the different types of love or different ways God gives grace to sinners or even identify the steps to asking for and receiving forgiveness.

Topical studies still need many of the same skills as a Textual study. It is crucial that for each passage, the author's message is properly understood and that context provides the foundation for how the topic under study is being addressed. Elements of the author's intentions, the audience and the contest of the writing still have an enormous impact on the actual learning that occurs.

In effect, you can think of a topical study as a "study of studies." Each time you look at your chosen topic in a passage, you will need to apply the core principles of the textual study. As the study progresses, you will assemble and integrate all the learning into the larger topic.

Study Method 6: Systematic Study

The final method of study we will consider continues to blend aspects of both the textual and topical study methods. The systematic study seeks to organize the truth of God's word and present it in an orderly or systematic fashion.

Systematic study organizes God's word into different topics and identifies the truth the Bible reveals about each of these topics. It also identifies how different topics relate to each other. The primary purpose of this type of study is to organize the knowledge gained from study in clear statement. In many ways, it brings a scientific-like discipline to studying and categorizing what God has to say.

A systematic study is similar to a word or topical study in that is uses the entire Bible to identify all teaching on a given systematic topic. At the same time, the systematic study must also be concerned with author, audience, and context to properly understand the message God was trying to communicate in any given passage.

Over the years, and through many studies, a set of topics have been established. They represent the core elements of what the Bible has to teach. Information is organized in a set of subtopics which cover the entire range of what we know about the greater topic.

Each of these systematic topics has a technical or scientific name. All the names end in the ending "ology" – which in Greek means "the study of". While the terms aren't often used in normal conversation, it's useful to have a high-level understanding of the terms.

Theology Proper: The study of God the Father

Because the entire topic of Systematic Study is often generically called "Theology" the study of God the Father is indicated by the word Proper – meaning literally "the study of God Himself".

Bibliology: The study of the Bible

We touched briefly on this topic in Chapter One where we looked at the inspiration, infallibility, and authority of the Bible. The full list of sub-topics is much wider than just those three items.

Christology: The study of Jesus Christ

The word "Christ" is Greek and means "the anointed one". Since Jesus came as the anointed one of God, this word is used instead of "Jesusology".

Pneumatology: The study of the Holy Spirit

The idea of breath or air characterizes the Holy Spirit. That's what the Greek word pneuma means. It's the same root word that gives us pneumatic (driven by air) today.

Anthropology: The study of Humans or Mankind

Just as in the scientific discipline of anthropology, this topic is concerned with human beings; who we are and how we relate to those around us.

Hamartiology: The study of Sin

In Greek, the word "hamartia" is an archery term and means to "miss the mark." It is the word in the original language translated as "sin". Because of this, the systematic term for the study of sin uses this root word.

Soteriology: The study of Salvation

Drawing from another Greek word, "soter" which means "salvation" or "savior," this topic looks at what is salvation, and how does it happen?

Ecclesiology: The study of the Church

On the day of Pentecost, the church began when over two thousand people believed in Jesus. This topic looks the church and organizes all the teachings of the Bible.

Angelology: The study of Angels

This topic looks at who the angels are and what they do?

Satanology: The study of Satan

This topic obviously looks at Satan or the devil. Who is he? Where did he come from? What does he do? What is his final end?

Demonology: The study of Demons

This is similar to Angelology, except with demons.

Eschatology: The study of End Times

The Greek word "eschaton" means "the end of all things". So eschatology is the study of the end of all things. Often this study also includes the study of prophecies that speak about the end of days.

You don't need to know or memorize all these words and topics. But sometimes it's nice to know what the big words mean. You can amaze your friends by using one in a sentence some day, or you can follow along as other Christians have a more technical conversation.

Living what you've learned

Now that you've read this chapter and learned a little bit about different kinds of Bible study, how does this impact how you live? This chapter might seem like it's just a bunch of information, but it was written to impact you today.

Take a moment and reflect on the questions below. Given what you've learned about the different method of Bible study how would you answer? Are you satisfied with your answers, or would you like to see growth in your life so that you could answer differently?

_____

Which of the study methods have you begun to use? used regularly? mastered? _____

_____

_____

What distractions lead you away from studying the Bible? _____

_____

_____

What is one bold change you need to make in your approach to studying the Bible? _____

_____

_____

_____

Chapter Three

UNDERSTANDING THE BIG PICTURE

N OW THAT WE'VE LOOKED AT THE WIDE VARIETY of different ways to study the Bible, we're going to zero in on one method for the rest of this book. Most people, when they talk about studying the Bible, think about a textual study. That's what the rest of the book will address by showing the six easy steps to study.

Before diving in, some questions need answers. The first and biggest question is what are you going to study? If you pick up your Bible, you'll notice that it's a large book. There are so many possibilities! Where should you start?

One possible approach would be to study the entire Bible. This is an admirable goal. However, for most people, this amounts to more material than they can effectively manage. It also creates a number of difficult challenges given the diversity of authors and audiences and types of writing. If you want to study the entire Bible, it's probably best to study it in its smaller parts, then combine them together to gain an appreciation of the larger volume.

If the entire Bible is too big, then you might look at the individual verses. That offers a much more focused target of study. Once again, this presents some significant challenges. The verse (and chapter) decisions were not a part of the original communication from God. They were added later for our convenience.

Small sections, like verses, can create challenges where the individual verse is part of a larger point. That larger point often adds context and meaning to the verse. Examining too small a segment of Scripture can result in a loss of perspective that defeats the point of the study.

For the purpose of this book, we are going to concern ourselves with the natural unit of study in the Bible: one book. Though the books range in size from very large (Genesis & Isaiah) to very small (Jude & Third John), many are of a size that makes them relatively easy to study. Later on, we'll put everything you've learned to use and we will study the book of Titus together.

There are several reasons that make the book an ideal segment for textual study.

1. **Single author and single audience**. In most cases, a book of the Bible was written by a single person to address a set of needs in a single person or group of people. As you will see shortly, understanding the author and audience is essential for understanding the message.

2. **Context**. Many books of the Bible were written as a single literary work. This means they build a specific context or purpose and organize the points being made around that purpose. Understanding that context is essential to properly identifying the message.

3. **Completeness**. We have confidence that the points being made by the author are complete. If they had more points to make, we would expect them to have written more. Knowing that we have an entire message brings confidence to our study.

Given that a book of the Bible is an ideal study, what book should you start with? My strong advice is to follow the KISS principle (Keep It Simple Silly). When you begin studying the Bible, start with a relatively short book. Shorter books are easier read and have fewer points to understand.

As you gain experience and skill in this discipline, you can expand your view to larger and more complex books of the Bible. This is actually another example of the milk-to-meat progression we discussed in Chapter 1. Begin simply and tackle more difficult challenges as your skill grows. There's no shame in this approach. It is practical.

It doesn't matter which book of the Bible you choose to study. You always begin the same way by asking the opening questions. These questions are simple to ask and will begin to lead you into the study of the material. Their purpose is to help you get a handle on the big picture of the book.

Who is the author?

As we've seen before as many as 39 men wrote books in the Bible. They were all very different from one another. They lived in different times, in different places and had different backgrounds. This will certainly show up in their writing styles, communication and the messages they have to deliver.

The first step of any study is to begin to identify who wrote the book. This will be important background later on as we dig in. This will also help us understand the author and get aligned with the message they were communicating.

What was the author's name? What facts do we know about their lives? When and where did they live? What kind of position did they hold in their society? Were they concerned with any issues in their day? What did they want to accomplish?

These are a few of the kinds of questions we want to ask. You might come up with more. That's great! The more you know the better you'll understand what's going on.

You might wonder how you're supposed to figure this out? If you don't know off the top of your head, how are you supposed to learn? The answer is simple: read.

The best way to find out about the author is to read what they wrote in their book. Almost every time they will reveal insights into who they are and what they are doing. This is the first step of discovery and learning.

In fact, all three of the Big Picture questions are based on reading the book of the Bible to find answers. Every time you begin a new study of a book of the Bible, you will want to start off by reading the book in its entirety to get the big picture. It will help you gain an understanding of who wrote the book and more!

Understanding who the author is can have a dramatic impact on how you study a book of the Bible, or even on what you expect to get out of the book itself. If the author is an authority figure, they will tend to communicate one way, but if they are a participant in the events they are describing, their approach may be more explanatory. These are the kinds of ways that the author sets the tone for how we study a given book.

Here are a few books of the Bible. List out what you know about the author of each of these books. If you don't know anything, don't worry, just leave that book blank.

Genesis: _____

Judges: _____

Psalms: _____

Isaiah: _____

John: _____

Ephesians: _____

2 Peter: _____

Let's take a quick tour through these books and learn a bit about the authors and see how that perspective colors our understanding of what they have to say.

Genesis was written by Moses. We don't learn a lot about him in this book, but he's introduced in quite a bit of detail in the book that follows: Exodus. There we learn that he was well educated, a military leader, and he was a Hebrew who was born in Egypt. But we also find out that he was the leader who led the children of Israel out of Egypt. He wrote the first five books of the Bible as a way to educate the twelve tribes about who God was, and the nature of the special relationship they had with God.

Judges doesn't exactly say who wrote the book. We don't have an author that we can look to in order to determine a perspective. Jewish tradition attributes the book to Samuel the prophet. Traditions do not have the authority of the Bible, so we have to accept that we don't know who wrote the book.

The Psalms were not written by any one person. It is a collection of poems and songs that the people of Israel used when they worshipped God. The psalms are often associated with David, the King of Israel. He wrote many of them. But many other men contributed to the list of Psalms. Each Psalm is attributed to the man who wrote it. But across the book, we see that the focus isn't on an author, but on God, the object of worship.

Isaiah was written by a man named Isaiah. We learn that he was of noble lineage, and lived during the time of four different kings in the southern kingdom of Judah. He tells us how he was called to be a prophet of God in chapter six, and what God told him that job would be like. Isaiah wrote in a time of prosperity, but when danger and threat were always just over the horizon.

John's gospel was written by John the disciple and close friend of Jesus. He went out of his way to make clear that he was there and saw everything first hand. Toward the end of his book, he explicitly stated that he wrote this book to convince people to believe in Jesus and thereby gain access to eternal life.

Ephesians was written by the Apostle Paul. He was a prominent Jewish leader in Jerusalem who had a dramatic conversion when he met Jesus on the road to Damascus. Much of his story is told in the book of Acts. In Ephesians, we see Paul's theological mind at work as he writes about what it means to be a believer in Jesus.

Second Peter was written by the Apostle Peter. Like John, he spent three years living with Jesus, listening, and learning. After that, he was a major leader of the newly established church in Jerusalem. What he shares in his second letter is based on this intimate knowledge of Jesus and what He taught as well as Peter's own experience as a pastor dealing with real-world issues.

You can see that each one of these books has a very different author. Their perspectives vary, and their experiences are uniquely their own. As we learn more about them, we are in a better position to be able to understand what they have to say in their books.

As you begin to study a book, you will become friends with the author. You'll learn their preference and tendencies. You'll come to understand how they like to communicate and what they do when they want to emphasize something. They'll tell you all this. You just need to pay attention to what they have to say.

Who is the Audience?

Just as the author matters to us as we study, so does the audience. Their identity gives us clues about what the book or a section of the book is trying to communicate.

Often the passage, or the larger book, will provide clues about the initial readers of the message. What do we know about them, their relationship to the author, the specific circumstances they were facing or their relationship to God? Answers to any of these questions will be invaluable in understanding what God is trying to communicate.

It's important to remember that when written, each book of the Bible served a critical purpose communicating something important to an audience. In fact, the needs of the audience may have driven the author to say what they did. The more we understand who the audience is, the better we can align with the message they received.

If the audience was a troubled church, we'd expect one kind of message. If they were the rebellious nation of Israel, we would expect something very different. If the audience knew the author personally, that would open up a more intimate level of communication compared to receiving a message from a stranger.

Just like with the author, the best way to understand the audience is to read what the book of the Bible says. Sometimes the author explicitly names the audience, whereas other times their identity is implied. Many times the author will describe the problem or reason that they wrote, which offers valuable insight into the character and needs of the audience.

Let's look at the same list of books in the Bible that we used before. Write out what you know about the original audience that first read the book. If you don't know anything, that's not a problem, just leave that line blank.

Genesis: _____

Judges: _____

Psalms: _____

Isaiah: _____

John: _____

Ephesians: _____

2 Peter: _____

Let's take a quick trip through these seven books and get a quick glimpse of the audience who which they were written. As time passes and you study more, this is the kind of information you'll know.

Genesis was the first of five books written by Moses for the people of Israel. They had been living in pagan Egypt for over two hundred years and needed to be reminded who God was and who they were in relationship to Him. The book of Genesis describes the covenant relationship between God and their forefathers: Abraham, Isaac, and Jacob. It also shows how God's providence brought them to Egypt, just as His power led them out.

The book of Judges continues the story of Genesis and the first five books. The audience is the same group of people – the nation of Israel. Judges describes the state of affairs after the time of the great leaders of the exodus and conquest of the promised land. The book of Judges is written to the nation of Israel in general, but it is about them as well, pointing out their tendency to do what they wanted to do rather than following God. While God always proves faithful to save them from foreign oppressors, the people are faithless and continually turn away from Him soon after He intervenes.

Psalms is another book that was originally written for the nation of Israel. It served as part of their worship guide. In it, we see their condition and their heart of faith and praise. But Psalms is also written to a second audience. It is written to God. Many of the psalms are actually the prayers of the psalmist directly to God. They highlight the author's faith and hope in God's goodness and justice. In this way, many of the psalms offer an intimate insight into prayer and worship.

Isaiah tells us that he was sent to deliver God's message to the people living in the southern kingdom of Judah. Throughout the book, these people are described as hard-hearted, turned away from God and interested only in their own affairs. This sets up some very dramatic messages as Isaiah points out the consequences of their self-reliance and lack of relationship with God.

John also tells us that he wrote his gospel for those people around him who did not believe in Jesus. At the end of the book he says that it was written for the purpose of convincing unbelievers that Jesus was the Messiah and that through Him, they can receive eternal life. Because of this, we can see that throughout the book he makes very plain the need for salvation and Jesus as the only savior who can provide it.

Ephesians was written by the apostle Paul to the church that was located in the city of Ephesus which was located on the coast of the Aegean Sea in what is modern-day Turkey. Paul knew them well, having founded the church and visited them on several occasions. From this close knowledge, Paul writes the kind of theological truth that they need to understand to grow in their faith.

Second Peter was written by the apostle Peter, but not to a specific location or group of people. Peter wrote his second letter to believers who had been scattered far and wide across the Roman empire. These believers were undergoing persecution and living in very challenging circumstances. Peter's letter was intended to be truth and encouragement in a variety of circumstances as it was taken around to many different locations and read to the believers there.

Just from this small sampling of books in the Bible, we can see that there is a wide diversity of people who were the initial recipients of the communication. Sometimes it was a very specific group with very specific needs. Other times it was a general group with similar needs. Finally, many of the Old Testament books were written to the nation of Israel to highlight the nature of their relationship with God.

As you can imagine, the audience has a significant impact on what the author needs to say, how they say it and how the logic of the communication is structured. As you spend the time to understand the author and audience, you'll be dialing in on the message of the book itself.

This leads us to the final question.

What type of literature is the book?

The Bible is composed of writing that draws from a wide variety of literary styles. As you read the books in the Bible, you will certainly notice how they are different from one another.

A poem is different from a letter, which is different from a historical account. You know this from your everyday life. A newspaper article is different from a tweet, which is different from a novel. Different literary styles have been developed to communicate different kinds of messages.

Different types of literature also use different techniques to communicate. If you were to write a love letter, you'd probably want to use flowery language that created word pictures of your love. On the other hand, if you were writing a how-to manual for a complicated task (such as assembling a dresser), you'd naturally focus on clear, specific, concise instructions with no flowery frills.

41

We naturally want to use a type of literature that is appropriate to the purpose we want to communicate. The writers of the Bible did the same thing. The Song of Solomon is love poetry. Ezra is a historical account of people and events. Colossians is a letter that was written to the church in the city of Colossae.

When you look at it this way, it seems quite normal for a Biblical author to pick a specific type of writing and literature to communicate their message. Since they lived a long time ago, their options were a little different than what we might choose today, but the principle is the same.

Across the Bible, we generally see six different types of literature employed. Often books of a similar type are grouped together to make a section that has the same style.

HISTORY

These books tell a story of what happened. They can be either relate what happened from a distance or be first-hand accounts of what a person did. These books tend to focus on a general audience as opposed to a very defined and specific group. Often the history books in the Bible give background and educate the reader on general principles. Very often, the history is centered around God and His relationship with a group of people.

POETRY

These books use picturesque language to communicate feelings or an internal state. This is exactly what you would expect from poetry. When books use this style they tend to be personal and relational rather than an explanation of historical or spiritual truths.

LETTERS or EPISTLES

Letters are generally written from one person to another, or to a specific group of people. They can be both educational and teaching in nature, or they can be very personal – depending on the relationship between the author and audience and the author's purpose.

GOSPELS

We give the name gospel to the 4 books which tell the story of Jesus' life on earth. The gospels are similar to history books in that they tell the story of Jesus' life and death. However, because these books present the message of salvation, they are given their own grouping.

PROPHECY

In the Bible, prophecy means "to speak forth". It doesn't always have to contain statements or predictions about the future. The prophets were men who were selected to speak directly for God, so in these books, we hear God speaking through these men to a wider audience. Sometimes the prophetic language is picturesque like poetry. However, because the words come directly from God, these books are grouped as Prophecy.

WISDOM

In ancient times "wisdom" was understood as the skill or ability to live a good life. That meant a life properly oriented toward God. In the wisdom literature, we see wise teaching targeted to instruct a person how to live well.

Take a look at the list of books below and see if you can identify what type of literature they use. If you don't know, that fine. Just leave that line blank.

Genesis: _____

Judges: _____

Psalms: _____

Isaiah: _____

John: _____

Ephesians: _____

2 Peter: _____

Genesis tells the story of creation and what happened thereafter. It is a book of history. God is the main character, and the book focuses on Adam and Eve and their family, Noah, Abraham, Isaac, and Jacob.

Judges is also a history book. It tells the story of the nation of Israel after they took possession of the land of Canaan. It's not a very happy history because the Israelites continually find themselves struggling to make good choices and require God to deliver them time and time again.

The Psalms are poetry. This is easy to see just by looking at the print on the page. It's all indented and appears very much like poetry. The types of poetry that were employed are different than those we see today, so don't expect iambic pentameter.

Isaiah is a prophetic book. In chapter six we read about how God recruited Isaiah to be His spokesperson and sent Isaiah to the people of Judah to deliver His message. Much of Isaiah features God speaking about what is going on in Isaiah's day. However, there are also sections that speak about events which had not yet happened such as the coming of the Messiah, and what He would do.

John is a gospel, written by Jesus' closest friend and companion. John relates what he saw of Jesus' life and ministry. He also relates many of the things that Jesus said. Matthew, Mark, and Luke also wrote gospels. They tended to be more chronological in their telling whereas John chose a more thematic approach.

Ephesians is a letter or epistle written by the apostle Paul. It was literally a letter sent to Ephesus and the believers there to share some things he wanted them to know but couldn't tell them in person.

Second Peter is also a letter. It was written by the apostle Peter and sent to the believers who had scattered across the Roman provinces to escape persecution. Both of Peter's letters were written this way and served to encourage those believers to hold fast to their faith, even though their world was being turned upside down.

The only type of literature that was not represented on our list was wisdom. The book of Proverbs is a wisdom book. It shares little nuggets of wisdom for how to live a wise, godly life. Job is also a wisdom book. Rather than giving specific advice, the story of Job's life is one of faithfulness to God. Job illustrates what the wise life looks like when lived well.

Laying a strong foundation

These three questions help us lay a foundation for our study. They begin to dive into the setting and the reason why the book of the Bible was written in the first place. They help us identify the need or problem that was being addressed. Finally, they give us tremendous clues about how the author will be communicating his points to the readers.

All of this information lays a foundation upon which we can build as we focus on the message throughout the study process. It sets a tone that helps us figure out what is going on as we read specific sections in the book.

Here's an example. Later on, in this book, we'll look at Paul's letter to Titus. We very quickly discover that Paul and Titus were ministry partners and Titus was providing leadership to the churches on Crete on behalf of Paul. Paul's specific messages to Titus reflect this relationship. He was very specific about what Titus should be doing and how it should be done.

Contrast that with Paul's letters to the churches in the region of Galatia. We know that Paul founded many of those churches on his first missionary journey. But now some time had passed, and the Galatians were struggling with some theological issues. Paul's letter was not to a ministry partner, but to struggling churches who needed correction and instruction. Instead of addressing ministry strategy, Paul called the churches out for straying from the gospel he had shared with them and reiterated the truth to which they needed to return.

I hope you can see the different tones that begin to emerge between the two books. They share the same author and literary style, but because of the audience differences, the entire tone of the book shifts. Indeed, if you were to study both books, you would find that they address completely different topics and approach the communication in a completely different manner.

I always recommend that new students begin by studying shorter books of the Bible. The best way to understand author, audience and literary style is to read through the entire book and see all the different clues that emerge. This is much easier to do in a six-chapter book than it is in a sixty-six chapter book. This doesn't mean the shorter books are easier or less important than the bigger books. It just means they are easier to manage and apply all the study techniques I will show you.

As you develop familiarity with these skills, you can tackle more challenging and larger books. The skills and techniques you'll learn in this book are suitable for tackling any book of the Bible. The only variable will be your skill, and experience, using the tools.

You took me out of context!

One of the main reasons for the three big-picture questions we've just discussed is that it helps us to set a context for the book we are studying. The Oxford Dictionary of the English Language defines context as "the circumstances that form the setting for an event, statement, or idea, and in terms of which it can be fully understood."

That's exactly what we want to maintain; a setting so that the message can be understood. This is one of the most important tools we have as Bible students. Once we establish context , we are in a position to be able to understand the message as it was originally intended.

Context is an important topic for the Bible student because so many of the skills and techniques we use in our daily life work against a proper understanding of the Bible. These are things that we do almost without thinking about. Often they are coping techniques for a lifestyle that has become flooded with too much information. However, the consequence is that we don't always properly understand what we are reading.

Take a look at the list below and see how many of these skills you use on a regular basis.

Skimming: _____

Partial Reading: _____

Sound Bites: _____

Multi-Tasking: _____

Skimming means reading over a text and not focusing or concentrating on every word, but rather looking for keywords which convey the general idea of what the writing is about. Often we can pick up the general idea of something by skimming. But we never get the full picture or detail of what is being communicated.

Partial reading happens when we read the first few lines or maybe a paragraph and then think we understand what the larger writing is all about. This is a common technique when we don't know if we want to read the whole piece. By reading a few lines, we can see if it grabs our interest and then we can make a decision about whether to read more or not. If we think the author has summarized their main point well enough, we may even decide we've read enough.

Sound bites are short, pithy, memorable phrases that stick out of a larger passage without accurately representing the full meaning of what the passage has to say. We see this in news reporting all the time. A headline may grab the most controversial or interesting sentence out of a thirty-minute interview. That one statement does not completely represent everything that happened in the interview.

Multi-tasking happens when we don't apply our full attention to what we are doing, so consequently, we only process a fraction of the information that is presented. Of course, we all think we're pretty good at multi-tasking. We use it all the time as a tool for managing the onslaught of information. While we use the technique, it still yields a limited understanding of what we are interacting with.

These skills and behaviors are commonly used as techniques to manage the onslaught of information being presented in our society today. With smartphones, computers and streaming media, we are bombarded with more information than we can reasonably handle. These skills are largely aimed at filtering out information we don't think we need to pay attention to.

When studying the word of God, however, we want to pay attention to every detail. How tragic would it be to hear from the Creator of the universe and only pay attention to a part of what He has to say? When He tells us how to please Him, we need to know all the things He desires. When He tells us what makes Him sad, we don't want to miss something and then turn around and do it out of ignorance. Therefore, focusing on context is an important practice.

Studying the Bible requires a new set of skills that help us pay attention to the full message that God has communicated to us. We don't want to miss a bit. And this approach begins when we start to address the Big Picture Questions.

Instead of filtering out information, we want to ensure that the entirety of God's word comes through. For the Bible student, the following skills are key to being able to hear all that God has to say to us today.

Deep Reading: _____

Reading Through: _____

Finding Context: _____

Dedicated Focus: _____

Deep reading is the opposite of skimming. It means that we read each word with equal attention and focus. It may be tempting to relax a bit when you think you understand what is going on and skim until you think something new is happening. That will be precisely the moment when you miss something important. Deep reading helps us stay engaged all the way through.

Reading through a passage means that we read all the way to the end. Just because we understand how a passage begins doesn't mean that we understand all the points that it is going to make. Choosing to skim is really choosing to miss out.

Finding context is the opposite of relying on sound bites. Context maintains the bigger picture of what is being said, by whom, to whom and considers the way that the message is being communicated. Any time we latch on to a catchy phrase as the representation for a larger passage, we begin to rip the message out of its context and lose focus on what it is trying to say.

Dedicated focus means that when we deal with the Bible, we are not doing anything else. It's not possible to study the Bible effectively while watching TV or having a conversation with a friend. It's also not effective if we are continually jumping over to our favorite social media site to check on what's happening. Dedicated focus means that for a period of time, this is the only thing we are doing.

It's all about the context!

Every time we study the Bible, we want to understand the passage in the context of how it was being communicated by the author to the audience. That is why the beginning of the study focuses so much on author, audience, and type of literature. These are the foundations of context and help us understand how we ought to approach the study.

Remember, back in Chapter One, you learned that the sender gets to determine the message they want to communicate. The receiver has the task of understanding what that message is and what the sender meant by it. Anything other than this is called miscommunication.

Here's a silly story that illustrates the importance of context.

> A young believer looking for wisdom in a difficult circumstance opened their Bible at random and picked a verse to read: Matthew 27:5b. Shocked they opened to another random verse: Luke 10:37b. Completely shaken they tried one more time: John 13:27b. At this point, the young believer was thoroughly confused and discouraged and did not know what to do.

Look at the verses the young believer picked at random:

Matthew 27:5b: [H]e departed, and he went and hanged himself

Luke 10:37b: And Jesus said to him, "You go, and do likewise."

John 13:27b: Jesus said to him, "What you are going to do, do quickly."

Ok. This is a ridiculous example. But it illustrates the dangers of what can happen when we lose focus on the context of the verses we are studying. When considered properly none of the verses above can be taken to suggest we ought to go and hang ourselves.

It's unlikely that if you did take a verse or a passage out of context you'd end up in such a crazy circumstance as that story. At some point, common sense would kick in and you'd reconsider what you were reading. But what about the situation where you miss context and the result still sounds reasonable? This is very possible, and in fact, happens every day.

Understanding context is essential to the message. Would you willingly choose to mess up a portion of the message God has for you? Not likely. No student wants to intentionally miss the point. That's why understanding context is so important. What was the author trying to communicate to the audience? Stick with this in your study and it will serve you well.

As we study the Bible, we're going to start to work these context-oriented principles into the process. We want to build a process which guides us into the correct understanding. It's unlikely that these anti-context skills will be eradicated from our lives. Therefore, we need to make sure that we train our minds to use different tools when the Bible is under consideration.

As I introduce you to the six steps of the study process, you'll see how we carefully build a framework of understanding that supports the correct context. All of the topics that we've addressed in this chapter will come into play and you'll be naturally guided into a correct and proper understanding of God's word. I just want you to be aware of the alternative, so you can be an active participant.

Living what you've learned

As we look at the process of studying the Bible, you can now see that it requires thought and a careful approach. How are you tempted to short-change your study of the Word of God? In what ways do you have practices that work against gaining a right understanding of what He has to say to you?

Take a moment and reflect on the questions below. Given what you've learned about the big picture and context, how would you respond to the perspective being voiced? Are you satisfied with your answers, or would you like to see growth in your life so that you could answer differently?

"Because I'm not skilled I won't even try." _____

_____

"Because I don't have a lot of time, I won't use good technique."____

_____

"I only want to study if I get feel-good messages in return." _____

_____

"I only want to study on my own terms, my way." _____

_____

"I want to study so I can get head smart."_____

_____

Something else? _____

_____

Chapter Four

TOOLS FOR UNDERSTANDING

CONTEXT ALONE WON'T REVEAL THE MESSAGE contained in the Bible. It's an important start but only lays the foundation. In order to really understand what the Bible has to say, we will use another set of tools that will make the message come alive.

The tools that we're going to dive into in this chapter are often taken for granted. They are actually things that you and I do naturally and unconsciously in our everyday life. Nothing I'm going to share will be new; it will all be a review.

As we go through these next tools, I want you to remember that you don't have to become a master in them in order to gain value. Your goal is only to become more aware of them. If you love language, then you can dive in and really absorb the technique. But if you hated English in school, use this as an opportunity to pick up one or two new concepts.

Many people who don't care for tools of language and grammar study the Bible very successfully. You don't have to be a grammar geek! But understanding a little bit about how grammar works will open up the word of God in amazing and surprising ways for you.

Because the Bible is delivered to us in writing, we use the basic tools of literature to discover what it has to say. These tools aren't strange or foreign. They are things we use every day of our lives. However, we most often take them for granted and miss the value that they offer.

Paragraphs: Contain one key thought which is supported by several sentences. We group sentences into paragraphs to effectively communicate and develop ideas to support the message.

Sentences: Come in different types which can be used to create different meanings. Not all sentences are the same and understanding the type of a sentence will help draw out the meaning it communicates.

Words: Keywords can unlock meaning and show us what the author had to say. Often the meaning the author is communicating is highlighted or showcased by specific words that we should pay attention to.

As adults, we generally understand the written word. We know how to read paragraphs, sentences, and words. We are familiar with how these building blocks can be used to create messages. This is foundational to communication in our daily lives.

When it comes to studying the Bible, our general understanding doesn't always serve us well. Often we don't use our knowledge to its maximum advantage, and so miss parts of what is being communicated. In this chapter, we will sharpen our skills around these tools so that we can dig deeper and understand more of what God has to say.

The tools we are going to look at in this chapter aren't difficult to understand or use. You probably learned about them in Junior High School. The odds are, however, that you haven't practiced these skills for a long time. They are there, but rusty.

Studying the Bible benefits the most from practice. Using these skills and tools over and over makes them much easier and natural to use. So as we begin, they may be a little awkward. You can expect that to change after you've used them a few times.

Paragraphs are the first building block

Did you know that when ancient writers wrote their manuscripts, they did not use paragraphs or punctuation? The original copy would have been received as a long block of text that the reader had to sort out as they read. Despite the lack of punctuation or formatting, they still followed much of the same structure that we use in communication today.

When translating into English, most translators apply standard conventions of English grammar, including the use of paragraphs and punctuation, even though they did not occur in the original manuscripts. This is done to help the modern reader understand what the writer was trying to communicate. Paragraphs are one of the benefits of an English translation of the Bible.

Most Bibles you can buy today will give an indication of paragraphs and paragraph breaks. There are two basic styles that are commonly used: verse-centric and paragraph-centric.

The verse-centric approach begins every verse on a new line, regardless of the paragraph or sentence structure in which it occurs. This means that each verse looks like its own mini-paragraph. The editors typically use another convention to indicate where a new paragraph begins. Often they will use a bold font for the verse number in the first verse of a new paragraph. If you have a verse-centric Bible, you will find an explanatory section in your Bible where the editor explains how to identify paragraphs.

The paragraph-centric kind of Bible follows a normal English format. Paragraphs begin on new lines, and sentences continue one after the other until a new paragraph begins. Verses are indicated by little verse numbers that are sprinkled throughout the paragraph. Those Bibles will look generally like this book.

Regardless of how your Bible indicates paragraphs, we know that a paragraph consists of several sentences that are grouped together to communicate one main idea. Most paragraphs have three parts: the topic sentence (what the paragraph is about), body sentences (which support the topic) and a concluding sentence.

This is the traditional structure of a paragraph. Not all paragraphs will have all three components. In some cases, a paragraph might have a topic and a conclusion, or maybe a topic and some clarifying body sentences. It's up to the author to decide how to structure the paragraph.

One thing we can be certain of, however, is that a well-constructed paragraph has one topic. This topic is what links together all the sentences that make up the paragraph. This is a rule of English grammar, but also a foundation of good communication.

When we were in school and were taught how to write in paragraphs, we were told to put the topic sentence first, then support it, then summarize it. Not all sentences in the Bible will follow this pattern. As the reader, it will be up to you to identify the topic by reading and using good sense.

- The paragraph may not lead with the topic sentence, so you may need to search for it.
- The topic may be implied but not explicitly stated.

This, then, becomes one of the first activities of studying the Bible. To identify what the author is saying, we need to understand the topics of the paragraphs that he has written. Not only does that help us understand the details of what every paragraph is about, but it helps us see the flow and development of ideas throughout the larger work.

A very common, and good, practice that some people do is briefly summarize the topic of every paragraph in their margin. This study technique draws them into the passage and drives them to understand all of the author's points. Once they have been identified and written down, they are available as an easy reference later.

We will talk about this idea of marking on your text a little later in the book. You don't need to start doing this right now unless you want to. I will make some suggestions for good ways to manage this that will help your study stay organized.

Once you have identified the subject of the paragraph, you have a pretty good idea what the author was trying to communicate. Each of the sentences in the paragraph should then support the main idea in some way or another. The way that the author develops or supports the main idea is key to understanding the message they wanted to communicate.

Because each paragraph is about one idea, it is helpful to break a large section of text, such as a chapter, down into paragraphs. This simplifies the process of focusing on what is being said to see the flow of topics or main ideas. Only focusing on sentences and words can result in too many pieces of information to keep straight in your mind.

There is a certain sense of freedom that comes when you realize that you can break a long complicated passage down into just a few paragraphs. Each paragraph then provides its own key points that the author is communicating. Suddenly something that is very complex or daunting can be simplified and made much more understandable.

Paragraph key points can also preserve the context we discussed in the last chapter. If you are working with a set of paragraphs, and you have identified the main point of each, you can focus on any one paragraph without losing the flow of what is happening around it. This will become very helpful later on when we start to dig deeper into what the author had to say.

It can be a useful tool to summarize each paragraph in a passage to capture its main point. This technique helps cut through the wordiness of the paragraph itself to identify the main points being made. I like to do this when I study the Bible because of how it can aid in creating clarity.

Let's take a moment to practice this idea of understanding a paragraph. Don't worry about finding the "right answer." This is about practicing the skill of understanding the paragraph. At first, it's often difficult, but as time progresses, it will become easier.

People who worry about finding the "right answer" tend to freeze up on exercises like this. We won't be grading anything, so don't worry about that side of it. Instead, let the text itself guide you and you will find good answers.

Read Acts 6:1-6 and answer the questions below

_____

What is the topic sentence? _____

_____

What are the supporting or body sentences? _____

_____

_____

What is the concluding sentence or result? _____

_____

_____

_____

How was that? Were you able to answer all of the questions?

When I read the passage, I think that verse three contains the topic sentence. It seems to be the instruction that was given. Verses one and two provide the background why the instruction was needed. Verses four and five explain how the instruction was carried out. Verse six is the conclusion where the Apostles blessed what was done.

Don't worry if you got a different answer. This is a practice. As you continue to do this over and over, you will become more skilled and more confident in your ability to break down a paragraph.

Not all sentences are the same

We all know that sentences can be quite different from one another. We use different kinds of sentences every day. Most of the time, we don't even think about the kinds of sentences we use. It's no different in the Bible. Biblical authors use different kinds of sentences.

For the Bible student, quickly identifying different sentence types is a powerful tool for understanding the author's message. While we may unconsciously understand sentences, making it more intentional is helpful to uncover the truth of what God has said.

Declarative Sentences

Declarative sentences make a statement. That is they assert specific items as truth. In this, they can be very simple sentences. Length does not take away from the power of a declarative sentence.

- The wages of sin is death.
- In the beginning, God created the heavens and the earth.
- The Lord is my shepherd, I shall not want.

Each of these is a declarative sentence. They make statements about different topics. We don't have to do anything with these sentences except believe that they are true.

Declarative sentences are a good way for the author to communicate information to the audience. They explain and describe what the author sees or understands, and communicate that to the readers. In this way, we find a lot of declarative sentences in the Bible. They are a staple of good communication.

Interrogative Sentences

Interrogative sentences ask a question. An interrogative question is different than a declarative sentence in that it expects some kind of response or reaction from the reader. Generally, we would expect it to be paired with some kind of answer.

Interrogative sentences are common in dialog, where one person asks a question of another person. When an interaction between people is being reported, it's common to see questions as part of the dialog. This is one way that a person's perspective is revealed.

The author can also ask specific questions of the reader. Of course, unless the author expected the reader to write back, an answer isn't really what they are shooting for. These kinds of questions are called "rhetorical" and they often imply or suggest their own answer.

- "What must I do to be saved?"
- The LORD is the stronghold of my life; of whom shall I be afraid?
- What shall we say then? Are we to continue in sin that grace may abound?

The first question above is asked by Nicodemus of Jesus in the gospel of John. What follows is Jesus' answer to the question. As a result, the question becomes the topic of the answer that follows.

The last two are asked by the writer and don't expect an answer from the reader. The answer is either implied or provided by the author himself. The first example is from the psalms and is a question that the psalmist doesn't need to answer. The answer is obvious: "I will be afraid of no one." The second example is Paul asking a logical question based on what he had been saying in a previous chapter. He goes on to emphatically answer the question: "By no means!"

In each of these situations, the question is used to draw out additional information. This is why we use questions in everyday life too. So as a Bible student, when a question is asked, pay attention.

Imperative Sentences

Imperative sentences give a command or an order. They are different from the other sentences in that they always expect something from the recipient of the command. Normally an imperative statement is looking for obedience or compliance.

We often see imperative sentences where the person speaking does so from a position of authority. In the Old Testament, leaders used this kind of language with their followers. In the New Testament, church leaders used this kind of language with the people in their churches. We even see Jesus using this kind of language.

- Be strong and courageous!
- Do not be conformed to this world
- "Follow me and I will make you fishers of men."

In the first example, God is speaking to Joshua just after he has just been selected to lead the nation of Israel into the promised land. It's a tough job and they both know it. But God steps in to tell Joshua what he needs to do. *Be strong and courageous* leaves no middle ground. It's an order and he expects Joshua to comply.

In the second example, Paul is writing to the church at Rome. He leads off this section with the command *Do not be conformed*. This is the most important point he is making, and he uses strong command language to get it across.

The final statement is Jesus calling his disciples. His command *Follow me* expects them to obey. The disciples have only two options at this point. Obey or disobey.

Whenever we run into an imperative sentence in the Bible, it's a clue that something is expected. Whether in compliance or in action or in a way of thinking, commands place an obligation on their recipients.

This is the author's way of communicating with their audience. It's a way to let the audience know that something is expected of them and that they need to take a specific action. Later on we'll learn how to translate these commands to ourselves, but for now, we can see that the author expects the audience to do something.

There is no real limit to the way that Biblical authors can use different types of sentences. This depends on what they have to say and the kind of relationship they had with their audience. It can also be influenced by the type of literature they choose to use.

For us, as we study the Bible, the different sentences can be a tremendous help as we search for the message being communicated. Often we use these types of sentences as patterns that help us zero in on the message we want to understand.

When reading the epistles in the New Testament, it is common to look for imperative sentences. These commands often form the main idea of what the writer is trying to get across. The sentences around can explain why obedience is necessary, what happens when the readers obey, or even what happens if obedience is withheld. Finding a command in the middle of a long paragraph can bring clarity to a passage which is otherwise confusing.

Another common Bible study technique is to look for questions and answers. In dialog, these are often important interactions between characters. In narrative styles, they are conventions that the author typically uses to bring attention to his main point.

Declarative sentences generally don't have such clarifying effects. However, as we begin to immerse ourselves in the text of Scripture, these sentences lay a foundation of truth that builds up and strengthens our faith. These sentences describe the world and our lives as God sees them. God's view often differs greatly from the natural view that we see.

A look at grammar and structure

Now that we've looked at paragraphs and sentences, the last stop in this chapter is to consider the words of the text. While every word is important because God spoke it, some words have a greater ability to help us zero in on what God has to say.

The Bible has over 700,000 words from Genesis to Revelation. That's a lot of words. Of course, they are divided into books and chapters, which helps to break that down into something more manageable. Many readers, however still find the text difficult to make sense of.

There are several factors that contribute to this confusion:

- The Bible was written several thousand years ago and talks about topics that aren't familiar to readers today.
- The culture of the writers and readers are quite different from contemporary cultures
- The types of literature and writing used in the Bible are not commonly used today

Focusing on paragraphs and sentences is a good way to begin to understand what the Bible has to say. Looking at specific words used is another technique to gain a deeper understanding of what the authors are trying to communicate.

Biblical authors use a few logical patterns to organize what they have to say. These patterns help simplify their message and make them easier for the reader to identify and understand. And yes, the words we'll consider here are key to identifying these structures.

What do I mean by logical structures? It's easy. There are three:

- **Contrast**: comparing 2 or more ideas and showing how they are similar or different
- **Summarization**: reducing a larger passage to a few concise points that have the same meaning
- **Conclusion**: the logical consequence or outcome of ideas which have been previously communicated

As you learn how to pick out these structures, you will quickly gain insights into what the Biblical writers were communicating. Fortunately, there are a few keywords we can use to quickly identify these techniques and help us dive into the meaning.

The first two words we'll look at are called conjunctions. Their purpose in grammar is to link together two or more different ideas. The key is how those ideas are being linked together. As we will see, they will either be linking two similar ideas, or they will be contrasting the differences in two ideas.

AND – More of the same

And is one of the most common words in the English language. We probably use it all the time in our everyday language. That doesn't change the fact that this simple little word has a very powerful meaning and function.

The word *and* joins together several ideas in a way that means "more of the same." How we look at one of the ideas is similar to how we look at the entire set of ideas. What is true about the first one, is probably also true about the second one.

Look at Matthew 6:11-13. Jesus is giving a model prayer, often called the Lord's Prayer. One part of the prayer reads "Give us this day our daily bread <u>and</u> forgive us our debts as we have forgiven our debtors. <u>And</u> lead us not into temptation but deliver us from evil." He uses the word *and* to link three main ideas:

STUDY THE BIBLE - SIX EASY STEPS

- Give us our daily bread
- Forgive our debts
- Deliver us from evil

Looking at the prayer this way, we can easily see that all three are similar in that they are requests being made of God. In each case, something comes from God to the person making the prayer. This is the similarity highlighted by the word *and*.

If I were studying this passage, I would probably summarize this specific section as "Three requests we can make of God". That's a great way help me see what Jesus was trying to say. Being able to summarize like this also helps bring the flow of ideas into better focus as I read through long sections.

Finding an *and* in the middle of a passage is an open invitation for us the readers to ask the question "How are these things alike?" In some situations, they will be obviously alike. In other sections, however, the similarities may be much more subtle and may require some additional thought or digging.

Some writers like to use what we would consider run-on sentences. When faced with a long sentence like that, it can be difficult to understand what the point is. Using the *and* technique (and the one I'll show you next) can simplify the sentence and bring clarity where you might otherwise feel lost.

BUT – Contrast, the Opposite

But is another common word you'll find in the Bible. It's a short word and flows off the tongue or pen very easily. But just like *and* from the previous section, it has a very important function.

Whenever you encounter the word *but* you know that you are dealing with contrast. That means the idea before the *but* is different from the idea that follows it. Look at how I used *but* in the previous paragraph:

- *But* is a short, simple word – just like *and*
- It serves an important function

You can see that I'm contrasting the idea of simple and short with the concept of importance. Small size does not mean small importance. In fact, the opposite is true. *But* is the word that allows me to set up that contrast.

Biblical writers use the same technique. They often use contrast to show the differences between different ideas.

- Righteous versus Unrighteous
- Saved versus Damned
- Holy versus Sinful
- Spirit versus Flesh
- Obedient versus Disobedient

The list of Biblical contrasts can go on and on. Let's take a closer look at Romans 12:2. Paul is at a turning point in the flow of the book. He's spent the first eleven chapters talking about how we cannot be righteous on our own and are reliant on Jesus sacrifice to be pleasing to God. In the five chapters that follow, he wants to discuss how his readers ought to live in light of that truth.

The statement "Do not be conformed to this world but be transformed…" is the point around which Paul pivots. Paul is emphasizing that transformation is fundamentally different from conforming to the world. Looking more and more like the world might be seen as change, but it is not the transformation that Paul wants his readers to pursue.

In effect, Paul is saying "Not the first thing but the second thing which is completely opposite!" Because of the word *but* we are able to see how Paul makes this pivot.

Not all buts are equally significant to the context of their passage. As you study the Bible, this is what you want to zero in on. Whenever you find a *but*, you should be asking yourself the question "What is being contrasted, and how are they different?"

Similarities and contrasts are two good things to look for when you study the Bible. They will guide you to understand what the author is trying to communicate. But they are not the only words to which you should pay attention.

The next set of words we'll consider are another grammatical structure called prepositions. They are also linking or comparison words, but they have a different set of meanings and purposes. In the cases we'll look at below, the words are used for summarizing or drawing conclusions.

BECAUSE – what follows is a consequence of what precedes

The word *because* highlights the relationship between two ideas or concepts. When one idea naturally leads to another, we're likely to use this word.

Because has explanatory power. It explains why something happened or is true. Often when this word is used, we can find a question that begins with "why" that this word will answer.

In the Bible, authors use this word so they can explain the why behind the ideas they communicate. It's a word that helps us get to the bottom of the matter.

When we come across the word *because* we know that an explanation is in order. We also know that what follows is related to what came before. It helps us tie together all the verses we are reading.

Consider Ephesians 2:4-5. Paul opens the chapter saying "you were dead in trespasses and sins." Verse four contrasts that idea with the word *but*. But what?

In this particular example, Paul sort of scrambles his ideas. With a little thought, we can re-order the words of verses four and five and make this flow a little better:

- But God being rich in mercy (4a) made us alive together in Christ (5b)
- Because of the great love with which He loved us (4b), even when we were dead in trespasses and sins (5a)

With this reordering, the meaning of the passage becomes much clearer. The reason why God made us alive is the great love He has for us. And that love was shown to us even when we were still unable to respond to His love!

The word *because* introduces the reason for the action. In this case, God Himself is the reason, and it's important that we see Him as the reason for the making alive in the passage.

I like the word *because* when I'm studying because it allows me to drill deeper into the truth that is being expressed. It gives me little glimpses of the deeper meanings of the Bible. It helps me ask the question "Why?" that is always lurking in the back of my head when I study.

FOR – Indicates purpose or the goal; with respect to, because, why

Another word that is similar to the word *because* is the word *for*. In some respects *for* is like a synonym of *because*. It has a similar meaning, and is often oriented around answering the question "Why?".

When we see the word *for* in our Bibles, we should quickly get the idea that a reason for something is being provided. Granted, we do need to step back and figure out what is being answered. An answer without a proper question is like a car without an engine.

We can see an example of this word just a few verses after our last example. Look at Ephesians 2:8-10.

- We have been saved by grace
- It is a gift from God, not from anything we have done
- So that none of us can boast
- *For* we are God's masterpiece, created by God
- We were created for good works which God has prepared

The word *for* picks up the statement that we should not boast about our new standing in God. We did not create this standing, God did. While we were created for good works, we did not arrange any of them, God did. Throughout this section, the Bible is pointing attention away from us and back to God.

THEREFORE – As a consequence of what came before

This is a great word in Bible study. Like the two that came before, this points to a summary or a consequence of what has come before.

When I was young, my pastor said that whenever we encountered the word, *therefore*, we should ask "What's the therefore there for?" In other words, stop and identify the relationship between the ideas being explained.

Therefore is a backward-looking word. It looks back in the text to the ideas that have come before. What follows the word is something that is true because those first things were true. Often the word leads into a summary or a consequence of earlier truths.

We can see this used in Hebrews 12:1. The writer to the Hebrews says "Therefore, since we are surrounded by so great a cloud of witnesses... let us run the race that is set before us." What's the therefore there for?

Since *therefore* points backward, we need only look as far as Chapter eleven. In this chapter, the writer shares story after story of men and women in the Old Testament who acted on faith. Indeed, they acted without ever seeing Jesus, the person in which they were placing their faith. If those men and women could live in faith without seeing, despite the opposition they experienced, then how much more should we, who have seen and know Jesus, be able to live by faith?

Therefore, then, becomes a pivot word transitioning from the stories of others to the story of us. It carries all the points that were made in the previous chapter and brings them to bear on the point the author is making for us.

Whenever I come across a *therefore* when I am reading the Bible, I circle it. It's one of those words that jumps out and tells me that an author point is at hand and that I should pay attention to it.

There are several other words that serve a similar function. You can look for them in the same way that you look for *because* and *for*:

- So
- So that
- Since

They share similar meanings to the words we've discussed. They really point to the author making a point that we need to dig into.

When you see them, be sure to pay attention and look around for how the author is linking ideas. In most cases, you'll be looking back and seeing how those points are being linked forward to a new idea that is being introduced.

REPETITION – Using a word over and over throughout a passage

The final grammatical tool we'll look at isn't a connecting word. It's a repeated word. Authors use repetition to bring emphasis and attention to an idea or a message.

When reading a passage, look out for words that are repeated. You might find a word or two that is used a couple times in a section of the Bible book you are studying. That's fantastic! Whatever that word is, it represents an idea that the author is trying to make prominent.

Sometimes you might read a passage and find one or more words that are repeated more than a couple times. That's when you know that you're looking at a major theme that must be reckoned with.

Grab your Bible and read John 15:1-11. There is one word in particular which is repeated several times throughout the passage. Write that word below:

_____

The words *vine, branch,* and *fruit* are all used multiple times in this passage, but they are not the word that most jumps out you. Jesus is talking and He wants to make a different point very clear.

I'm talking about the word *abide.* Some translations may instead use the word *remain.* How many times is it repeated in those eleven verses? Go back and count them.

I count ten different times that Jesus uses this word in the span of eight verses. That's a lot! Do you think that Jesus is trying to make a point about abiding/remaining? Yes!

In John 14, Jesus tells His disciples that just as events are building to a climax with the religious leaders, He's going to be leaving them. It makes complete sense that the very next thing that He says to them is to remain in Him. If they scattered and ran and refused to remain, then the gospel would not have been spread to us. I'm glad they got the message!

In this chapter, we've looked at a few different tools that we can use to understand the message God communicated in the Bible.

Paragraphs – Each paragraph communicates one main idea. The sentences of the paragraph work together to support the main idea.

Sentences – Different kinds of sentences have different kinds of meanings and implications for us. We need to pay attention to the sentence selection as we study and use them appropriately.

Words – It's effective to focus on connecting words. They help us identify the point that the author is making, by showing contrast or similarity or by linking ideas together.

You might love this attention on grammar or you might hate it. The goal is neither to love or hate it. As I said at the beginning of chapter three, these are tools that everyone can use.

As you continue to learn about studying the Bible, these are the kinds of tools that will become familiar. This just means that you'll learn how to use them effectively. They have great value for helping you understand what God has to say to you.

As we get farther into the book, I'll suggest some techniques that might make this part of the study more interesting or fun. When I study my Bible, I break out colored pencils and pens as a way of making this relatively dry topic interesting and fun.

Living what you've learned

In this chapter, we've shifted gears from big ideas to more detail-oriented items. For some of us, this is a really big transition and may force us to dust off skills that have lain dormant for years or even decades.

Take a moment and reflect on the questions below. Given what you've learned about paragraphs, sentences, and words, how would you answer the questions provided? Are you satisfied with your answers, or would you like to see growth in your life so that you could answer differently?

_____

Studying God's Word means digging into a deeper level of details. What would hinder you from doing this? _____

_____

_____

A few tools were illustrated in this lesson; what would prevent you from learning more tools (e.g. grammar) so that you could better study God's word? _____

_____

_____

What rewards could you receive for pursuing this kind of detail in studying God's word? _____

_____

_____

_____

Chapter Five

APPLYING WHAT YOU LEARN

U P UNTIL THIS POINT IN THE BOOK, we've been looking at tools to understand what the Bible has to say. I hate to say it, but understanding is not enough! If we stop here, we will miss out on the most important part of the Bible study process.

For the curious person, understanding might scratch that intellectual itch. Getting that itch satisfied is a good feeling. But it stops short of the ultimate promise that we have in the Bible: Life Change.

Yes, if you remember all the way back to chapter one, we are studying the Bible because it is the word of God. It literally contains the words that God wants us to know. The creator of the universe is talking… are you listening?

Listening is a start, but we need to take action on what we hear. As we understand the truth God is communicating, it will inevitably call for change in our lives. I'm not under any delusions that I'm living a perfect life. I doubt you are either. So I think it's reasonable to say that each one of us has some area that needs to be changed and improved.

This change that is calling out to you may take a lot of different forms. There is no "one size fits all" application of the Bible to an individual life. This is the part of the study process where you will get to decide what actions are necessary and appropriate.

In all likelihood, there will be some form of confession – agreeing with God that what He says about Himself and about your life is true. That's the essence of confession. Change can only begin when we get on the same page as God.

You may also be called to do something differently. This could take the form of starting to do something you've not been doing or stopping something that you have been doing or even changing the way you're doing something today. In either case, studying the Bible results in a visible change in your life.

Sometimes the application demands that you believe something to be true. We don't often talk about our beliefs. They tend to be quiet, under-the-covers kinds of things. But beliefs influence everything we think, do and say. What you believe about gender and sexuality, political philosophy, rights and responsibly, individuals and groups impact the way you view and value people in society around you. The beliefs determine the ways you prefer to interact with people. They deeply influence the things you think, but do not say aloud.

As you study the Bible, you may need to change what you believe about yourself, or God, the church, or possibly the person next door. You might be challenged to think through new ways of believing and how that really influences your life and what you do next.

This is the point of change, and it's the reason for studying the Bible. We want to submit to God's perspective and allow it to permeate our lives. The only way to know what that is comes from studying what He has told us. The only appropriate response is to align with what we have learned.

Change isn't easy. There's no better way to say that. But we do have a secret weapon. We have the Holy Spirit who is working in our lives. As we apply the Scripture we have studied, we are cooperating with the Holy Spirit to bring these changes about.

Change requires power. Change requires will. Change requires energy. The Holy Spirit supplies all of these. Not only that, the Holy

Spirit knows what we should be like, so He is also involved in the process of hearing God's voice in Scripture. Truly, the Holy Spirit is our secret weapon in studying the Bible!

So given that the goal of studying the Bible is to apply it to our lives, how do we do that? Do you remember the example a few chapters ago about the young Christian to found three passages at random and they seemed to be saying to go hang himself? Is that how we should be applying what we study?

Fortunately, there is a method for applying the Bible that allows us to understand what we should do as in application. This method will help us deal with situations like the hanging passages. It will also help us deal with passages seem to have nothing to do with us or our lives.

By way of overview of what's to come, the Bible study method goes through four repeatable phases which are intended to answer a final question: How should we live?

1. **Message Identification**: What was the author trying to communicate to the original audience?
2. **Audience Mapping**: How much is the original audience like me?
3. **Message Mapping**: Which elements of the message are relevant to me?
4. **Action Planning**: What do I need to do in response?

Most of the book up until this point has been focused on the first step: Message Identification. This step lays the foundation for everything that follows. If we don't properly identify the message, then no amount of application can get us back on the right track.

The remainder of this chapter will be looking at the three steps of the application process. Each of these activities is unique and discrete and represents a well-defined task that you can do, and check off as you go through the study process.

Audience Mapping

During the Message Identification phase, we spent some time identifying the audience. We absorbed everything we could about who they were, what they were like, the kinds of problems or needs that they had.

When we map the audience, we build on that information. Mapping the audience answers a specific question:

How much and in what ways is the original audience like me?

It's a given that there will always be a number of ways that the original audience is different than you or I. For one, they lived at least 2.000 years ago. The world has changed a lot since then! These kinds of changes are exactly what Audience Mapping is designed to address.

When we look at the audience, there are several different divides that we want to understand:

- The Gospel Divide – how did the audience relate to God?
- The History Divide – how long ago did the audience live?
- The Culture Divide – How is their culture different than ours?

Our goal as we map the audience is to measure the size of each of these main divides. Armed with that knowledge, we can understand how to adapt the message to apply to us today.

Let's dig a bit more into each of these divides so we can see what we're dealing with.

The Gospel Divide refers to the way that the individuals related to God. Some of the audiences in the Bible related to God through the rules of the Law. They couldn't receive forgiveness for sins, they could only cover them up with sacrifices that had to be repeated over and over again. They could not relate to God directly. They had to engage the services of a priest to intercede with God on their behalf. Given this kind of relationship with God, what they needed spiritually was different from someone who lived after Jesus' sacrifice.

As a general rule, the books of the Old Testament are written to audiences who did not have the benefit of understanding how Jesus would make a way to have a direct, forgiven relationship with God. They did not understand how they could become co-heirs with Jesus and have a completely new standing before God.

In the New Testament, we see new kinds of audiences with respect to the Gospel Divide. Starting in Acts, we see how the gospel went forth and changed people. These people were able to receive complete forgiveness and have their standing with God completely changed.

The Gospels provide an interesting bridge between these two groups of people. While the audiences were often believers themselves, many of the stories were presented with Jesus engaging with people who did not have a redeemed relationship with God and viewed the legal requirements of the Mosaic law as the norm. So as we look at the Gospels, we can see that there are several different Gospel Divides that we should be aware of.

As we think about measuring the Gospel Divide between ourselves and the original audience, remember that the smaller the divide, the more directly we can apply the message to ourselves. We'll look at this in more detail shortly. But that's why we're going into such detail on this topic.

The History Divide refers to the fact that the farther back in time we go, the less like us people tend to be. Whether by virtue of language, situation, form of government, role or lifestyle, ancient people are less like us today than were people living in the first century Roman times. Even then, we must recognize that the first century was 2,000 years ago, so "similar" is a relative term.

The Books of Moses (the first five in the Bible) were written to a nomadic, tribal group of people who had just escaped slavery in a foreign land. By and large, that doesn't map very well to our situations today in the 21st century.

The history books of the Old Testament were written to people who largely lived in a monarchy. Their ideas of authority and proper civic duty were influenced and defined by the times they lived – and this would have influenced how they understood what was being written to them.

Hebrew or Jewish audiences in the Old Testament also lived under the historical reality that they were God's chosen people. They were chosen in an exclusive way that separated them out from all other nations and people groups of their time. Things could be said of them that were not true of the nation over the border.

This is different than the choosing which we experience today as followers of Jesus. Our choosing is individual, crossing all national, ethnic and people group lines. Their choosing was national, based upon the details of their birth into the Jewish nation.

These historical details can be subtle, but we need to bear them in mind. It may not be clear on the surface how this will impact our application. But I guarantee that if you continue to study the Bible, you will encounter situations where this kind of divide will have a real bearing on your application of the message.

The Cultural Divide is similar to the History Divide in some aspects. This divide recognizes that the original audience lived in a time that had a different culture than what we have today. There are many dimensions we could use to explore the Cultural Divide; we'll look at a few here.

One of the differences is that much of the Bible is written to an audience who lived in an oriental culture. The setting for the Bible is the Middle East, and that region has an oriental culture. This will show up in the idea of "wisdom", or in how arguments are made.

As a general rule, our notations of wisdom today are heavily influenced by the Greeks and the idea of intellectual wisdom. In ancient times, a wise person was one who lived well. When this comes up in the Bible, living well is seen to be one who lives well in a way that pleases God. Throughout most of the Bible, the wise person is the one who has a right understanding of themselves and God and lives a life that pleases God. This is in contrast to our current understanding of the wise person as the one who has the answers or can tell us what to do in a given situation.

A second area where culture comes into play is in the way that arguments are made. Western logic is linear and cumulative. That is, we make points as assertions and if/then arguments and link them together to build an argument. In oriental culture, arguments are made by telling stories or by making a given point a lot of different ways. We need to understand this difference as we could otherwise miss how an argument is being conducted.

If you want a really good example of this kind of logic, look at God's answer to Job in Job 38. The whole book of Job is a set of arguments between different people on Job's terrible situation. The big question is whether Job sinned and is receiving just punishment for his actions. Throughout Job maintains that he did not sin, and he does not know why God is doing this to him.

Finally, God interjects and speaks to Job. God asserts His glory and dominion, not through rational points buy by making the point an overwhelming number of ways. In this one chapter, God asks Job twenty questions which only God could answer *Yes*. The point is that neither Job nor his friends are qualified to stand in judgment on God, His actions or His motivation.

That is an extremely compelling argument! Twenty times, Job is forced to concede, "No I can't do that, I'm not on your level." Even though God didn't make the point the way we would, we can still understand what He is saying.

Another key element of the Culture divide is the difference of cultural practices. Throughout much of the Bible, slavery was a common cultural feature. Today we pride ourselves on having set slavery aside and fight it wherever it raises its ugly head. Where discussions of slavery occur in the Bible, it simply acknowledges that slavery is real because it was a well known cultural institution.

Because the Bible talks about slavery does not mean that we should be practicing slavery today. This is one example of a big difference between the culture of the Bible and the culture today.

Slavery is not the only cultural practice that is different today. If you look there will be many differences between the culture of the original audience and our culture today. And depending on where you are reading this book, there may even be cultural differences between you and other readers. That's fine. Applying the Bible has a way to deal with this.

As we do Audience Mapping, we are interested in identifying how much the original audience is like us. This then forms the basis or the foundation of how we draw the application and plan for action in our own lives.

The main principle of Audience Mapping is that the more the audience is like us today, the more direct we can make the application of the message that is being communicated. When the audience is different, then we have to adjust the message, without changing it, to apply to us today. When I put it that way, I think you will agree this sounds like common sense.

This idea of audiences which are different from us should not be a strange concept. If you've ever had any interaction with children you've experienced this first hand. While children may be similar to us in many ways, they are also different. Their ability to use discernment and judgment is quite different from ours. This influences the way we communicate with them.

When communicating with children, we often shape our message in a way that we would not if we were talking to an adult. Often we are very black-and-white with children because that's what they need: "Stay on the sidewalk." We want to be clear to a child in a way that they would readily understand. However, as adults, we communicate with each other differently because our understanding and experience are different than that of a child. We understand that the street is dangerous, but are able to use our adult judgment to determine if stepping into the street is safe.

As we look at Biblical audiences, we will see that the author communicated to them in a way that was appropriate for their situation. Understanding how the author communicated is key to discerning their situation, and then determining how that message will apply to us today.

Let's practice a little. I'll provide a series of passages from across the Bible. Read the passages and fill in the blanks with how the original audience is similar or different from us. You can use your general Bible knowledge to help with this, or just look at the passage, which will contain clues about the original audience.

Leviticus 16:1-10 _____

_____

Psalms 1:1-2 _____

_____

Matthew 4:12-17 _____

_____

John 3:16 _____

_____

Galatians 5: 16-24 _____

_____

Let's review these audiences

In Leviticus, the original audience is the children of Israel as they are wandering in the wilderness, waiting to enter the land of Canaan. As audiences go, they are pretty far from us today. Historically, they are very far removed. Spiritually, they are under the Law, this passage is actually all about the rules and restrictions for a single priest to approach God once per year. Culturally they are also quite removed from us. Their religious practices are different, their sense of government and authority are quite different, and their sense of being settled in one place of their own is also very different.

In the Psalms, the audience is still ancient Israel. They are living in their own land, under the rule of a king, but that is unlike anything we experience today. They also are still subject to the rules of the Mosaic Law, although this passage does not directly reference it.

This Psalm seems to be written to "the people of God". In this respect, we have something in common because while the exact details of the relationship may vary, this seems to be focusing in on how the people of God are living under God's rule.

In Matthew, we jump ahead to the New Testament. Matthew is writing to the Jewish people of his day, showing Jesus to be the promised Messiah. There is less of a historical gap between us and the audience than we saw in Leviticus. But there is still a cultural gap as most of us are not Jewish and none of us alive in a first-century Roman province. However, we also can see that this is the beginning of the presentation of the Gospel, so that starts to bring the message closer to us today.

John is similar to Mathew in terms of the historical timeline. We are looking back nearly two thousand years to these events and the audience. We also know that John is writing to prove that Jesus is the Messiah, and cause people to believe in Him. John's audience is different from Christians today, but he is presenting the gospel, which is a message that is directly relevant to us today. In fact, there are people all around us today who do not believe who need the gospel – and this passage is very appropriate for them.

Finally, Paul in writing to the people of the region of Galatia (in modern-day Turkey), is addressing people who in many ways are like us today. They are believers, they attend church, and they have been influenced culturally by Greek and Roman ideals. We can't do anything about the two thousand year time gap, but as far as audiences go, they are about as similar as we are going to find.

Mapping the audience is critical because the original author tailored their message to the specifics of their audience. If that audience is quite different from you and I, the message will be crafted in a way that doesn't speak directly to us today.

Once we have mapped the audience and know the ways they are similar to us and different to us, we can move on to the next step in the application process.

Message Mapping

The process of message mapping is the process of adapting the message from the original author to the original audience so that it is appropriate to us today. This process follows some very specific principles that we need to review together.

Principle 1: You can't change the message.

Message mapping does not give us the freedom to make the Bible say anything we want. God is communicating with us. As the ultimate author of the Bible, it's up to Him to determine what the message is. When we step in and change it, we are ultimately usurping God from His rightful place. Nothing good ever comes out of that.

Principle 2: If the original audience is very different from me, I can apply general principles.

This is a key concept. This is why we went through the effort of understanding the original audience and mapping them. Imagine an Old Testament command to travel to Jerusalem and make an offering for sin. The audience here is an ancient Israelite who is bound by the law of sacrifices. Without the covering of the sacrifice, their sin remained unaddressed. This is completely foreign to a believer today. It would not be appropriate to read a command like that and think that we needed to go to Jerusalem and make a sacrifice.

This is a pretty obvious scenario. I chose it on purpose for that. As you read through the Bible you will find clear instances like this, but you'll also find other, more subtle differences that require you to stop and think about it.

Under the guidance of Principle 2, we would look at this command and say that the original audience is very different from us today. So we would identify an indirect message that applies to us today. This indirect message would need to be consistent with the original message but would be broad enough *that the details of the message are relevant to both us today and the original audience.*

This is an important concept. Backing up a message means that we make it less specific and more general or abstract. We don't get to change what it means, but often we are looking for the messages which sit behind the original message and make it true or lend it weight.

In the example I used above of being commanded to go to Jerusalem and make a sacrifice for sin, we could back up the message to say:

- Sin is a problem that needs to be addressed
- It's God's prerogative to decide how to address sin
- Give God His due of obedience and worship

Do you see how each one of these is true, both for the original audience and for us today? All I've done is backed them up, or looked for the principle underlying the direct message. This is how we get past the differences between us and the original audience.

These three statements draw out different aspects of the command. The first focuses on the problem of sin and points out that it demands some kind of action or response. The second focuses on God's right and ability to dictate the actions to address sin. The last one focuses on the human obligation to respond to God's command in obedience and worship.

If you were to study Leviticus, where commands like this are common, you would still be able to map the message to one of these three higher level messages and proceed with your application. None of these mapped messages violate the original message, and they all avoid the specific differences between the original audience and us today.

Principle 3: If the original audience is very similar to me, I can apply the message as it was communicated.

By contrast, when the original audience is very similar to us today, we can apply the message just how the author intended for the original audience. Consider Paul's exhortation to "Pray without ceasing" to the Thessalonians. The Thessalonians were believers like we are today. Yes, they are separated from us by time and culture, but those differences aren't relevant to the command.

It would be completely reasonable to conclude that since we are so close to the original audience, the command applies directly to us today and doesn't need to be backed up at all. We also ought to be continually praying just as Paul instructed the Thessalonians!

Principle 4: If the original audience is neither distant nor similar, I can apply general principles and specific messages

This is the part that might be a little tricky. What if the original audience has some things that are very similar, but some things that are very different? How should we apply these passages?

The first thing to do is to look at the message. Does it apply to the parts of the original audience that is similar or dissimilar to us today? If the message relates to an aspect of the audience that is similar to us today, then we can apply the message directly. On the other hand, if the message applies to the aspects of the audience that are very different from us, we need to map it so that it can apply to us.

Let's look at the Psalms as an illustration. The Psalms were the choir book of the nation of Israel. They were songs and poems that were used in the worship of God. The audience was the nation of Israel, who is quite different from us today. But as tools of worship, they are similar to things we do today in worship.

When the Psalmist says "Bless the Lord, O my soul, and all that is within me, Bless His holy name!" (105:1) we can apply that very directly because as a song of the worshipper, it holds very true for us today. We are also worshippers, and this is the truth about our unchanging God. The form of worship and the nature of our relationship aren't involved with this kind of worship.

On the other hand when the Psalmist says, "I was glad when they said to me 'Let us go to the house of the Lord.'" (122:1) he was referring to the Temple and the ceremonies which were performed there. This is quite distant from us today. We do not need to go to a specific place to worship God, nor are we constrained to specific ceremonies or sacrifices. In this case, we are much more distant.

We might generalize "the house of the Lord" to become "the place where we worship", and recognize that it is good to go into the presence of the Lord, regardless of where our feet might be standing at the moment.

This is an example how we might need to look at the audience in a more textured approach than just once for the entire book or passage. We need to recognize how we might be both close and far from the original audience depending on the specific command or passage.

Not every book or passage will have this kind of distinction. As students of the Bible, we need to pay attention as we study and not get locked up in one way of thinking. Our goal is to continually be reviewing the passage to find the principles which allow us to best and most accurately apply the message to our own lives.

Principle 5: Pick and Choose carefully!

Whenever human judgment is involved, there is also a temptation to pick and choose. Since you're being asked to map the audience and the message, you could be tempted to pick something you think you already do, or you could choose something easy to comply with.

Resist the temptation! The goal of studying the Bible is not to find the easiest way to comply or to make ourselves look as good or mature as possible. The purpose is to find out what God has to say to us today.

As you find situations where the original audience is quite different, you'll need to map the message. Your goal is to find the mapped message which is fully supporting and true in the original message and fully true today.

Don't let this intimidate you. With practice, you'll become much better at doing this. This is a good reason for studying with a partner because as you share your mapped message, you'll have someone else to hold you accountable. You'll also get an opportunity to see how someone else looked at the material and did the mapping.

In the next chapter, we'll consider additional resources that you can use to supplement your study process and help you with some of these mapping activities.

Let's practice again. Look at the passages below. They are the same ones we used to map the audience a few pages ago. This time read them and look at given the audience mapping, what would be an appropriate way to map the message as well.

_____

Leviticus 16:1-10 _____

_____

Psalms 1:1-2 _____

_____

Matthew 4:12-17 _____

_____

John 3:16 _____

_____

Galatians 5: 16-24 _____

_____

_____

Let's review the messages.

In Leviticus, the audience is pretty far removed from us today, and the message about how to atone for the sin of the nation is pretty deeply interrelated to those differences. Therefore, I would recommend backing this message up a bit. We could use the same mappings about the seriousness of sin, God's prerogative to decide how to deal with sin, or our obedience in following God's instructions. Additionally, in this passage, we could see God's holiness on display in all the ritual needed for the high priest to even approach Him.

In Psalms, we can treat the audience as "the people of God" and make it pretty close to us. In this case, the message can be very directly applied. The person who delights in God and refuses to conform to the wicked ways around them is blessed, literally happy. This message seems to focus in on the holy lifestyle of God's people, which we can take as something very relevant to us today.

In Matthew we see Jesus presenting the gospel to the people surrounding him. The context of the audience here is those who do not believe in Jesus. His command to repent is still timely today. Only through repentance do we come into relationship with Him. His claim that the Kingdom was at hand seems to be centered in His physical presence before them as He spoke. This might be something that we map into "Jesus has brought the Kingdom of Heaven to us". Here we acknowledge the passing of time but are still able to map the message. All of these mappings (both near and sort of far) remain consistent with the original message and allow us to apply them today.

In John, Jesus is also presenting the truth about the gospel. He is explaining it to Nicodemus, a Jewish leader who is seeking to know Him properly. The message to Nicodemus and John's first-century audience is the same as the message to us today.

In Galatians, Paul is giving commands to the Galatian churches how they ought to live. The Galatian Christians are generally close to us. They are removed by time and culture some, but the instructions here are about spiritual matters. In this, we are very similar to the Galatians. We can apply the commands directly and use the lists of the fruit of the Spirit and the fruit of the flesh as tools in our own lives.

The gospel changes everything

The gospel is the central theme of the Bible. From Genesis to Revelation, the entire Bible is either pointing forward to or looking back on the power of the gospel. As we read and study the Bible, it pays to notice how our study intersects this greater message of the gospel.

This trick is especially useful in sections that may not have an obvious or apparent relationship with us today. If we can see how the story of the gospel is being told, we have an important connection to what is being said.. Maybe we only get a glimpse of part of the gospel. Perhaps it is more fully in view. Either way, we know that this the central message of the Bible.

- How does the gospel resolve the central spiritual problem that is being described?
- How does the gospel radically alter our relationship with God (possibly resolving a problem being described)?
- How does the gospel give us the power to respond differently?
- How does the passage reveal our need for the gospel in our lives?

Linking into the gospel helps us see how God's plan of salvation is unfolding and how today we are such blessed recipients of His grace and mercy. As Christians, we cannot emphasize enough how radically the gospel changes everything.

Big sections of the Bible are narrative. They tell a story of individuals and groups of people. We have the option as we study to see how the gospel shows up in those stories, or how those stories illustrate the lack of the gospel. Often these stories are a perfect foundation to see the change that the gospel brings to our lives.

So what is the gospel? If we're looking for the gospel in our passages, it pays to know what constitutes the gospel. As believers, this is foundational to our faith.

- By nature, we are sinners and are always dedicated to opposing God. Consequently, we are separated from God and cannot reach Him on our own.
- Jesus came as a human and lived a sinless life. He fulfilled all of God's righteous requirements entitling Him to a full relationship with God.
- On the cross, Jesus took our sin paying the penalty of death and separation we deserved.
- In exchange, God credits Christ's perfect obedience to us and restores our relationship with Him.
- All we have to do is admit that we can't make our way to God on our own and accept the sacrifice that Jesus made on our behalf.
- Finally, God gives us a new heart and Holy Spirit power to love and obey Him, not reject Him.

This is fantastic news and the Bible points to this truth over and over. The more we see the gospel in the Bible, the closer to God's heart we come.

Plan for Action

No application is complete until we plan for action. It does us no good to understand what God has to say to is if we don't ever put it into our lives. This means that we need to take action on what we learn and discover.

As we look at the application, there are a few things we need to keep in mind. Where God commands, we must obey. Where God forbids, we must avoid. What God likes, we must like. Finally, what God hates, we must hate.

These four statements form the basis of our action plan. Where we find commands that apply to us today, we are on the hook to obey them. This is equally true for positive (do) and negative (don't do) commands.

In the same way, when we see the heart of God on display either in His likes or dislikes, we are to align with them. Throughout the Bible, God is revealing Himself to us. We need to pay attention to this and make it a part of our own lives.

It's tempting to give intellectual assent to something we find in the Bible. In so doing, we essentially nod our heads and say "that is true." But we don't really every internalize it or do anything about it.

Read the following passage and see what James says about people who are confronted with the truth and the two possible responses:

_____

James 1:22-25 _____

_____

_____

_____

James starts off with the principle: "Be doers, not just hearers!" He offers an illustration of someone who looks at their face in the mirror and doesn't react at all but leaves and forgets. Would you look at your hair in the morning after your shower and just shrug and walk away? Heavens no! You stop and take the time to fix it properly.

By the same token, the person who looks into God's word (James calls it God's perfect law of liberty) and walks away without doing anything about what they see is just as crazy. To see and know what God wants for us and from us means we need to put it into practice.

For some people, action planning comes naturally. For others, it's more work to think this through. Given what's at stake, it's worth a little effort to make it happen.

Most action planning begins with questions. As we consider the questions and answers emerge, the actions take shape. You can start your action planning with questions like this:

1. What am I doing that God's word forbids?
2. What am I not doing that God's word commands?
3. This passage describes what God likes. Where in my life am I doing this? Where am I not doing it?
4. This passage describes what God hates. Where in my life am I doing this?
5. If I fully embraced the message of this passage, how would my life look different tomorrow? Who would notice?
6. What are 3 things I could do this week that would illustrate the truth I just learned?

These are just a starter set. You can get creative with what you ask. The point is, you want to get specific. What are the specific things that you need to focus on? When will you do them? How will you know that you've done them?

This is the exact opposite of intellectual assent to the truth of God's word. Instead of being mental and idealistic, this is action-oriented and specific.

I would encourage you to write down your action plan. If it just exists in your head, it won't last very long. As soon as you go to work or watch a movie or play a video game, it will get pushed out and won't be effective any longer. Writing it down makes it permanent and real. You can come back to it and assess yourself against what you said you wanted to do.

Sometimes you'll find that the actions you need to take are hard. You'll find that natural human tendency to put off undesirable or difficult activities – indefinitely! Through all of this, we are looking for ways to make a specific action for change and growth.

Don't forget that you have the power of the Holy Spirit in you if you have surrendered your life through the gospel. The Holy Spirit provides both motivation and power to do things which please God. That means that the Holy Spirit is your ally in putting this application into practice.

As you look at obeying what you've learned, remember to pray. Pray for a change in your life. Pray for a softened heart that accepts the truth. Pray for courage to do what you know you need to do in obedience. Pray that God through the Holy Spirit will give you the power to see the change through.

You aren't alone in this either. It's very helpful to have a study buddy. That's just a person you study with. You may do the work together. You may discuss the results of the study you each do individually. You may share your action plan with them so they can follow up with you. Partnership is a great tool for making what you learn stick.

Above all, just start. It's easy to get stuck while making plans for something. Sometimes the plans end up becoming a substitute for what you've planned. Don't fall into that trap.

One of my favorite quotes sums up this idea. It's from W.H. Murray, the leader of the Scottish expedition to the Himalayan Mountains.

> "Until one is committed there is hesitancy, the chance to draw back, always ineffectiveness. Concerning all acts of initiative or creation, there is one elementary truth...that the moment one definitely commits oneself, then Providence moves. too. All sorts of things occur to help one that would otherwise never

have occurred. A whole stream of events issues from the decision, raising in one's favor all manner of incidents and meetings and material assistance which no man would have believed would have come his way

"Whatever you think you can do or believe you can do, begin it. Action has magic, grace, and power in it."

I think this advice is also true about studying the Bible. Begin. If you don't know how it will all work out, that's fine. As you go you'll start making decisions and the study will proceed. You'll stumble across something that captures your interest and draws you onward, until, before you know it, you've done it. If you've been filling in the blanks or answering the questions along the way, you've already begun!

By the end of this book, you'll have an opportunity to do a study with me. Make a decision now about how you want to encounter God's word and what you want to do to make it real in your life.

Remember, the application is the point of the entire process of studying. As we learn what God has to say to us we want to put it into action. If we don't, then God's word has no power to change our lives and make us more like Jesus.

Application can be hard, though. You might find a subtle resistance in applying the Scripture to your life. There is probably a part of you that wants to be left alone and not transformed.

Whenever you feel this resistance to applying what you've learned, it's a sign that the application is more important, not less important. When we think we've got it made on our own, we're in danger of the sin of pride that says we're ok just as we are. When God's word encounters that spirit of self-sufficiency, it will bring a message that challenges us.

When that challenge arises, listen to the promptings of the Holy Spirit who is in you. He will remind you of your sinful nature and the wonderful provision of a new nature and new power through Jesus sacrifice on the cross.

Living what you've learned

This chapter introduces a lot of new ideas. It takes what has been largely an academic exercise and brings it to where the rubber hits the road.

Consider the questions below as you reflect on the material in this chapter. These questions may help you find areas where you are liable to take shortcuts or shy away from the full power of applying these truths into your life.

This is just for you. Pray and answer honestly to see where you stand.

What is the percentage of energy you spend identifying the meaning of a passage vs. applying it to your life? Is that the right split? _____

_____

When you find an application, do you take it to heart, or just brush it off as inconsequential? _____

_____

After you study the Bible, how much energy do you spend trying to take action on what has been applied? _____

_____

Chapter Six

USING RESOURCES WISELY

ONGRATULATIONS! YOU'VE MADE IT THROUGH all the hard material. This chapter is going to focus on pulling all the ideas of the first five chapters together into a simple six-step process. We'll also talk about different resources and how you should use them.

At this point, a lot of people are geared up and ready to go. They want to know what God has to say to them in the Bible. Others lack confidence in themselves and so they focus on shortcuts to the answer. Perhaps they just read the notes in their study Bible. Perhaps they get a commentary on what they want to study and read what someone else has written.

To both groups, let me just say this: Studying the Bible is not a race. It's not a contest to see who can get to the message at the end in the shortest amount of time. It may seem like faster would be better, but it's not.

One of the key benefits of studying the Bible is the study process itself. It may seem difficult and confusing and you might not get to an answer as quickly as you want. That's ok. The process of wrestling with God's word will pay dividends in your life.

The application you make will be many times more impactful if it represents work and effort to arrive at it. So don't think that you are wasting your time. You're not!!

Think about it this way. If you wanted to eat a fine meal, where would you go? To a fast food restaurant where you can have your meal within moments of ordering it? Or would you go to a fine dining establishment where you might spend ninety minutes or more in a gourmet experience?

The fast food scenario might get you nutrients faster. But if we get down to it, that's seldom a real consideration in terms of our eating. Most people aren't in a race to get calories or they'll die.

The same is true of our spiritual lives. Our primary issue generally isn't that we don't know enough fast enough. Most people actually struggle with issues of follow-through and obeying what they have learned. Rushing to learn something but still not doing anything with it is functionally useless in our spiritual lives.

Instead, think about the gourmet experience. Even better, what if you had gone out and picked all the vegetables used to make the meal that day. Eating that wonderful meal wouldn't just be an experience for your taste buds. It would involve all of you, your time, effort and taste.

I'm not suggesting that you should go off and pick vegetables for your local fine dining restaurant. I am saying that things are different when you've put the time and the effort in yourself.

Bible study is better if you've spent time wrestling with the text to understand what it means. You're much more likely to remember what you've learned if you put effort into it. The message is going to impact your life much more deeply if you are working with your own study notes and conclusions than if you just pick up someone else's.

You won't be efficient or proficient at the beginning. That's ok. No one is when they start a new venture.

Skill at studying the Bible will come with practice. And that means continuing to study even when you just want to get to the answer to the question, "What should I do?" This is a normal part of the journey.

If you lack confidence in your conclusions and applications, that's normal and to be expected. Keep doing what you're doing, but find a Bible study partner where you can share your findings with them and discuss how they could be improved or corrected. It's nice if that person is a little more experienced than you are – then they can provide tips and hints along the way.

Whatever you do, don't fall into the trap of looking up the answer in an external resource because you are not comfortable studying for yourself.

Throughout this book, we've explored the different tools you have at your disposal to understand for yourself what God is saying to you through the Bible. Did you notice that not once did we talk about study Bibles or commentaries?

The truth be told, many people believe that studying the Bible means picking up a study Bible and reading the footnotes. We are blessed to have such a wealth of resource at our fingertips today. It's a blessing and a real problem.

Because these resources are so available, it's tempting to just use them as the first step in the process. When we do that, we cause a couple problems for ourselves.

1. We get answers, but don't have an effective understanding of why they are the answer.
2. Our spiritual development remains stunted in a "milk" state rather than progressing to the more mature "meat" capabilities.
3. We cripple ourselves for those times when the resource is not available.

I think a major reason for spiritual unfitness in the world today is that we treat ourselves to spiritual fast food rather than doing the work required to eat well. We probably don't intend for that to happen, but the temptation for convenience is great.

Take a look at how the Bible talks about the process of studying and learning what God has to say to us today. This is taken from 2 Timothy 2:15. I'm just pulling the first statement, and giving it to you a variety of translations.

- Be diligent to present yourself approved to God (NASB)
- Study to shew thyself approved unto God (KJV)
- Do your best to present yourself to God as one approved (ESV)
- Work hard so you can present yourself to God and receive his approval (NLT)

What image or picture does this verse present for what it takes to really know what God has to say to us today? _____

_____

_____

I don't know about you, but the idea of work and effort really jumps out at me. Even the Bible recognizes that this study process will require some time and effort. It sort of reminds me of the kind of work I had to do back when I was a student in school. That might not be a happy memory, but that's what it takes to realize the benefits that studying the Bible offers.

It is a proper biblical expectation that studying will take effort and energy and time. Only with much practice will it appear to be "easy". All the practice, however, will not be visible to those who think it's easy. But when that happens, the difficulty will have just moved to another level and new challenges will present themselves as old challenges are overcome.

I don't say this to discourage you. I want you to have an accurate expectation of what this process is like. I'm not saying that you need to be prepared for hundreds of hours of study time to get one little truth. You can effectively study the Bible on reasonable time investments.

Six Easy Steps to Study the Bible

This is what you've been waiting for: the simple six-step formula. I'll share it in summary form, then we'll dive into each of the steps and give it a deeper look.

1. **Read the text:** Establish the author, audience, and context
2. **Read the text**: Identify the author's message
3. **Identify questions that you want to answer**: Use your resources to find answers.
4. **Read the text**: Identify the author's message
5. **Map the audience & message**: Apply the message to your life
6. **Compare your conclusions with others**: Use any differences to expand your understanding

Did you notice that three of the steps involve the same action: Reading the Bible? That's because there is no way to study the Bible without spending time reading it. As you study, you will return again and again to the text to see what it has to say.

Let's take a deeper look at these steps.

Step 1: Read the text to establish author, audience, and context

The first time you approach a new text you'll want to do a surveying read. The goal here is to understand who is involved; that includes the tone the style and the kinds of topics being addressed. You'll want to see if the passage is long or short and how the author chose to use their words.

I always advise that during this first read, that you focus on marking or writing down everything the author reveals about themselves and about their audience. When you read with an eye toward this, you'll discover all sorts of little nuggets.

The author may use terms of endearment to describe their audience. They may refer to shared experiences that they had. They could reference problems that they know are going on and which need to be addressed They may cite parts of their own background that have a bearing on the points they make.

If you can gather all this knowledge together in one location, it will be gold later as you start to sort out the meaning of the passage and map the audience.

The first read always addresses author, audience, and context. It may be a single read. You might find it beneficial to read through a couple times to make sure you get it all. That's a great strategy, but it's up to you how many times you want to do this.

Step 2: Read the text to identify the message

This time though you'll be looking to understand what the author was trying to communicate to their audience. This read through is what we spent Chapter 3 and Chapter 4 discussing. Using the tools of paragraphs, sentences, and words as well as literature type and context you'll assess the message that the author wanted to communicate.

During this step, it's not uncommon to start to break the overall text down into smaller units for this step. In the study of Titus that follows, we'll study one chapter at a time. This helps manage the amount of information to try to understand. In other studies I've done, I've broken it down even farther – all the way to a single or small group of paragraphs.

The bottom line is this is where you will get into detail. It's effective to reduce the scope of what you're looking at as you try to glean out every little bit of meaning. Of course, you need to keep the overall context and flow of the entire text in mind. So from time to time, you might want to refresh your memory by reading the whole thing.

Odds are you'll spend sixty percent or more of your time on this one step. That's normal.

Step 3: Identify questions that you want to have answered

Up to this point, you've only been dealing with the text under study. There's been no opportunity to pull in study Bibles or commentaries or other resources.

Given that you're going off of your own knowledge, experience and the text by itself, there will probably be some questions which you'll need help to answer. This is perfectly normal and to be expected.

This is the point in your study where you can branch out and use other resources. In doing so, however, there are some guidelines that will help you get the most out this process.

First, wait until you get to this point. Resources are not an "as you go" kind of tool. We want to give God's word the first say in forming your opinion and impressions of what the text is communicating. It's fine to bring other resources, but wait until you've gone as far as you can before consulting them.

Secondly, ask questions. "What does this mean?" is not a legitimate question. Questions are intended to help you so that YOU can identify what the passage is about and what it means.

Just because we're bringing resources into play now does not give you the freedom to read every piece of commentary on the text you're studying. Resources are used to answer specific questions that arise out of the text which we cannot answer with our personal knowledge.

- When was this written?
- What does that word mean?
- Who is that person and what did they do?
- What is the audience's greatest need?
- What else was going on when this was written?

The best approach is to craft a specific question. This question will lead to research specifically intended to answer that question. Believe me, it can be difficult to actually form the question if it relates to an issue you don't understand very well. But don't let that deter you!

You'll get better research if you know what you're looking for. It will also help you design what you want to know and help you fill in gaps in your understanding of what the author is trying to say.

I actually encourage writing out your questions. You'd be surprised by how much clarity that alone can bring to the uncertainty. You'll find that sometimes just the process of writing it out will bring the answer to mind before you even start looking elsewhere.

The really big benefit of the question is it tells you when to stop using your resources. When you answer the question, you can stop. If the question isn't clear, you may just keep reading other sources until you run out of other material to read.

It might seem that maxing out on resources is a good thing. But it might not be as good as you think. When we started out on this process together we discovered that the purpose of studying the Bible was to discover what God has to say to us. This is different than reading a load of resources about the Bible.

There is such a thing as too much information or information overload. It's possible that you could fill your head with information that doesn't help you answer the questions you identified and which crowds out the words of God. We want to avoid that.

The goal here is not to learn everything that is possible to learn about a particular section of the text. The goal is to understand enough that we can determine the message that was being communicated and then start the application process.

This is why we want to keep our use of resources limited to the specific questions that we have identified. This way we're not overloading ourselves with information that is competing with the true purpose of what we are trying to accomplish.

Step 4: Read the text to identify the message

This seems like a repeat of step two and in some ways, it is. The main difference here is that now we have answers to the questions we identified. At this point, with questions answered, we should be able to complete the process of identifying the message.

In complex texts you may need to iterate through steps two, three and four several times. This is not a problem. However, in most studies, you won't need to go through these steps multiple times.

At this point in the study, you should be able to write down the points that the author is trying to make. The message should be clear enough that you can summarize it in fewer words that the original author used to communicate it.

Summarizing can be hard. I've met a lot of people who find it challenging to try to boil a paragraph or two down to a single concise sentence that captures the main points of the larger passage.

My only advice in this situation is that you should try. It may be hard. You may not think you've done a good job. That's not the measure of success. Success is found simply in doing it. The next time you try, it will probably be a little bit easier. And again after that.

Writing out the message in your own words is a great way to test how clearly you understand what the author is trying to say. It will force you to think through priorities and through word choice to make sure that you have truly found the most important elements to communicate. I strongly encourage this practice.

Step 5: Map the audience & message to apply to your life

This is exactly what we spoke about in the last chapter. No study is complete without an application to your own life. I strongly encourage you to write out your application. This creates a much more accountable result and allows you to review the application later when you review your study.

I have dozens of studies that I've done over the years. It's interesting to go back over these studies and see what points of the message were relevant and needed to be applied to my life. It's both an encouragement and an ongoing challenge to see this.

Step 6: Compare your conclusions with others

I strongly encourage you to study in pairs or groups, just because of this step. It is encouraging to be able to share your findings with others and see what they discovered. Often you will see things the other person missed and vice versa.

The process of sharing your discovery and application helps to make it more real in your own life. If you study alone it's much easier to shrug off an application and simply do nothing with it. However, a partner or group can offer a great accountability function that adds a lot of value to the process.

Not everyone has a partner or a group available. That's not the end of the world. If this is you, take heart. You can still have a very productive Bible study experience.

Instead of sharing your findings at the end of your study, you could get a commentary from a respected Bible teacher and read what they have to say on the passage you just studied. This is a powerful way to find nuggets you might have missed, or benefit from their greater learning.

This step is always saved to the end because the goal of studying the Bible is for you to go through the process and draw your own conclusions and applications. You will find that studies done this way are significantly more impactful than just reading someone else's study.

In my opinion, the end of the study is the best location to use commentaries in the study process. If you introduce them much sooner, they will tend to shape what you see in the passage to the view of the commentator.

While the commentator may be more learned and skilled than you are, validating their leaning is not the objective of your study. If you use the tools I've shown you and follow the process laid out here, you will arrive at good and valid conclusions and applications on your own.

An Overview of Resources

Let's talk a bit about resources. You may be reading this thinking "What kind of resources is he talking about?" I want to walk you through a few very useful resources that you can use to help your Bible study flourish. These will become the tools of your craft as you move into the next phase of studying the Bible.

You don't have to spend a lot of money to be well equipped to study the Bible. Some of these resources are free and are available to you right now. Others of these resources would be ones you might need to purchase. However, these tools aren't very expensive and could even be purchased over time to spread out the cost.

Pen & Paper – High Impact Basics

Believe it or not, the simplest resource is probably the one you'll use the most. I'm talking about the staple basics of pen and paper.

Get a fresh look at the passage by copying it into your favorite word processing application. Use the formatting to give it wide margins and generous spacing. Then read over it a few times to get the sense of what is being said. Use paragraph format so you can group together the main ideas and supporting text.

I'm not joking when I say to do this. In almost every study I do, I use this technique. It serves several ways.

1. It keeps me from reading the notes in my study Bible before it's time. This keeps my focus on the test of the passage itself.
2. I can create enough space to make notes, circle words, draw lines and generally keep all my notes together with the text.
3. I can be as messy as I want without impacting my study Bible.
4. I use regular printer/copier paper, so it's sturdy enough to withstand wear and tear.
5. Often I will spread out several pages so I can see them all at once. This can be challenging if the passage I'm studying splits over two pages in my study Bible.

When I do my own copies, I've found the following formatting to be most useful:

- Double spaced text with at least 1.5 inches on each margin
- 12 point font (no need to squint) and paragraph formatting
- Keep verse numbers in the text – this is helpful when you need to use references later.
- Print chapter numbers with the word "Chapter" so you can keep track of where you are in the book.
- Remove all other headings and summaries
- Put page numbers on the document in case you get pages out of order (it happens every time to me).
- Put a header with the Book of the Bible on the document so you can easily see what it is later.

By itself this is easily the biggest tool I use when I study the Bible. I usually go to an online Bible and find the translation I like and copy/paste the test into my own document.

Then bring a pen or pencil to the passage. Jot down questions that occur to you while you are reading. Just put them in the margin. Highlight important or repeated words. Sometimes they will show a pattern throughout the text.

I actually use a set of colored pencils. I've found that color helps me quickly recognize trends and patterns as I'm going through the passage marking things up. Over time I've developed some patterns that are consistent so when I read I can easily recognize some things.

I also keep a few pieces of blank paper available. On one I tend to write down a legend for all my markings. If I use a red heart every time I see the word "love", I'll write "Love" on my key and put a red heart over it. This helps me remember what colors and markings I've used so I can remain consistent. It's also useful if I return to a study I did a year ago, and I used something outside my normal pattern.

Sometimes I use these extra sheets of paper to build out charts and pictures that help me organize what I'm reading. If I do this, I always keep the pages together so that they are available later when I come back to the study.

Using this marked-up copy of the text is very useful later when you want to review your notes. If you have written questions and answers and ideas and inspiration on the document, you'll be able to remember what you were thinking during the study.

A Good Study Bible is Helpful

As you start to study the Bible, you'll soon discover that a good study Bible is a treasure trove of information. Whether you are looking for help on a specific passage, or if you want to expand your knowledge of Bible study, your study Bible will have a great set of tools for taking you deeper.

- Cross-references
- Maps & Diagrams

- Book overviews/introductions
- Resource materials
- Notes, explanations & commentary

Take some time to review all the reference materials that are available in your study Bible. Don't just look within the text of the Scripture. Most study Bibles have helpful information at the end or beginning too.

Most study Bibles focus on providing explanations and background to clarify the text. However, there are also specialty study Bibles that provide more targeted information. A good example of this is called an Interlinear. It displays the English text alongside the original Greek or Hebrew text. Since most of us don't read Greek or Hebrew, the editor cross-references the original language words to a dictionary so the reader can gain a deeper understanding of what the original language meant. Sometimes this can provide a deeper context on a passage that is confusing.

When it comes time to invest in a study Bible there are a few things to take into consideration. The most important point is what translation you use. When translators bring the text into English, there are several different techniques they can use.

- Word for Word
- Idea for Idea

The word for word approach is the one that serves best in a study Bible. This also goes when you copy the text of your passage into your own copy. You will want to use a translation that holds to this translation methodology.

In a word for word translation, the translators try to stay as close to the original words of the Bible. This is the most literal way to translate the Bible. It gives you, the reader of the English translation, the best picture of what the original words were. Since God is communicating them, they matter.

The downside of a word for word translation is that it might not read as smoothly as other translations. This is because the translators are limiting themselves to the words that the original author used.

In an idea for idea translation, the translators are looser. Their goal is to ask "what was the author trying to say here?" Then they use an English phrase which says that. It might not use any of the same words as the original. It will definitely include a lot of the translator's opinion of what the passage meant.

Since we are seeking to understand what God has to say, we want to eliminate as many steps that take us away from the original words. It's inevitable that we have some distance because our English Bibles are translated from Greek or Hebrew. But we want to keep it as close to that as possible.

Translations which I would recommend fall into this list:

- English Standard Version (ESV)
- New American Standard (NASB)
- New International Version (NIV)
- American Standard Version (ASV)

All of these translations will provide you with a reasonably literal translation of the Bible that ensures you're working with the words that God originally communicated.

Invest in a Bible Dictionary

A Bible dictionary is exactly what it sounds like. It's a dictionary of Bible words. If you are reading through your Bible and come across a term or a character that you've never heard of before, a handy Bible dictionary can help you get a definition.

Do you want a brief biography of Naaman? An overview of the Galilee region of Israel? A summary of the Babylonian conquest of Jerusalem? Or perhaps an explanation of what is a synagogue? A Bible dictionary will have entries on all these items that will provide you with a brief background and overview so you can better understand them as they occur in the passage.

A Bible dictionary is a resource that allows you to look up a huge variety of different Bible words in an alphabetical listing. You'd use it just like you would any other dictionary.

This resource is nice because it's well suited to answer the questions you document in step three of the study process. It will fill in the background that you never knew, and do it in a way that doesn't require a lot of work.

Another nice thing about the Bible dictionary is that it will give you the facts and not much more. There are very few topics where the dictionary will delve into interpretation kinds of information. This means that you won't be subtly led into a specific line of interpretation as you work with Scripture. The Bible dictionary keeps it pretty factual and informational.

The other benefit of a Bible dictionary is that it's alphabetical. This means that if there are other related words that are spelled slightly differently, you can find them above or below the entry you looked up. This can help set a context for a specific word that you're trying to understand.

Get a Bible Handbook

A Bible handbook is different than a Bible dictionary. The handbook will be organized by book of the Bible, typically in the same order, they occur in your Bible. The handbook doesn't focus so much on individual words as it does on the background and history of a given book.

When you use a Bible handbook you'll find a lot of relevant information about the history, author, audience, setting, timeframe, and purpose of a given book. This occurs in a general background section that helps the reader set a context for the book.

Many Bible handbooks also contain a chapter by chapter summary of the book itself. Each chapter summary points out key themes and points that are made and offers some interpretation and application of those points.

In many ways, the Bible handbook combines some of the benefits of a study Bible's introduction to a given book, with a light commentary on the contents of the book. This can be a very useful resource that will help you get oriented for your study.

Let me offer a word of warning. The Bible handbook may have assumptions about the contents of the book. Treat these portions just as you would a commentary and save them for step six of the process, not step three.

You might find some overlap between a Bible dictionary and a Bible handbook. If a word is a key to the book or passage, you may be able to look it up a Bible dictionary and see an explanation in the Bible handbook. You should recognize that the dictionary will explain the term in a neutral way, not regarding the special context of the location where you encounter it. The Bible handbook will provide the background in light of its application in one particular book or passage.

Don't be surprised if you find slightly different treatments of the same topic between the two different resources. Each one has a different perspective that it is bringing to the table. It's up to you to decide which one will best answer your question.

I like to use the Bible handbook book introduction after Step 1 to gain additional perspective on the author and audience and the timeframe of the writing. That helps me situate the book in its correct setting and better understand the people involved.

You might want a Systematic Theology reference too

This is the most optional of all the references I've presented. From time to time, you'll begin to dig into a given theological topic such as grace or salvation. If this is important to your study, it could be helpful to get answers about the broader scope of the topic.

We briefly discussed systematic theology in chapter two. There are dedicated books which offer a listing of the various "ology"s. These are the set areas of theological study. If you ever find yourself digging into specific theological topics, this resource might be helpful.

I would also offer a word of caution on this resource. It will almost certainly engage in some kind of interpretation of different passages and their meaning. If you are hoping to make up your own mind, this might be a resource best reserved for step six.

Would you like links to some good references?

On my website, I've made a list of reference I recommend. I'll give you a couple options for each different type of reference. If you're looking to build out your library, or just increase your tools for studying the Bible, start here. It will give you a good frame of reference.

https://www.Dennis-Stevenson.com/StudyReferences

It can be a lot of fun to build out your own study library. You don't have to cover an entire wall with volumes. Owning just a few key resources can dramatically enhance your study results.

The Internet is not a Resource!

While the internet is tempting and easy to access, it is the breeding ground of heresy, ignorance, misinformation and bad theology. Sure it's got some great references too, but can you tell the good from the bad?

The internet is full of people you do not know, who have not been verified or validated. Their theology and teaching have not been tested and found to be good. You do not know whether you are getting truth or lies from them. Assume lies.

While it may be tempting to use a search engine to look for information on the internet, this is not a valid study strategy. All of the materials recommended in this course have been reviewed and found to be trustworthy. The same cannot be said of resources found on the internet.

Unless you receive a recommendation from a mature believer, you should be skeptical about anything you find there.

I can recommend a few websites that are useful for accessing online Bibles and other study resources. These websites have well-established content that is generally safe to use. I'll be honest, I mostly use these sites to quickly look up verses when I'm studying. As a general rule, I still use the books listed above as my main reference sources.

- Blue Letter Bible http://www.blb.org
- Bible Gateway http://www.biblegateway.com

Wrapping it all up

Let's briefly summarize it all so that you can see the process. At the end of the day, it really is quite simple and straightforward. The hardest thing you'll have to do is trust that something so simple can bring the results you're looking for.

Here are the six steps again. Read over them and think about what you read in this chapter.

1. **Read the text:** Establish the author, audience, and context
2. **Read the text**: Identify the author's message
3. **Identify questions that you want to answer**: Use your resources to find answers.
4. **Read the text**: Identify the author's message
5. **Map the audience & message**: Apply the message to your life
6. **Compare your conclusions with others**: Use any differences to expand your understanding

At the end of the day, this approach is about giving you the tools to study the Bible for yourself. You don't have to rely upon commentaries, other believers, your pastor or anyone else.

Of course, you need to accept that you'll struggle first. Anything new is unfamiliar. That's normal and to be expected. Challenge yourself to push through this and you'll be surprised at the results!

Even better, keep reading. We're about to jump into a study of Titus together. This study will give you a chance to start practicing all the skills we just discussed. I'll guide you through by doing the study as well. I'll walk you through each of the steps and make sure you know exactly what to do, and then I'll share my study notes with you.

You can do it. I know you can! Just take the next step!!

Living what you've learned

Here are some questions to get you thinking about how you've studied the Bible in the past and how you might be tempted to try to shortcut the process. Read through the questions and give your answers. The goal is to not let your past limit your future. Will you commit to change and grow?

_____

Consider the recommendations above; how many of them have you violated while trying to study God's word previously? Will you commit to change? _____

_____

Do you have a good set of resources at home that will support an effective study of the Bible? Will you commit to expanding your resources? _____

_____

A six-step approach to Bible study was laid out. Will you commit to using it to study a passage of the Bible in the next two weeks? (hint: you can keep reading and use the study I've provided) _____

_____

_____

Part Two

USING WHAT YOU'VE LEARNED

Chapter Seven

AN INTRODUCTION TO TITUS

NOW THAT YOU'VE LEARNED THE SIX EASY STEPS, let's practice them together. The next four chapters will take you through the book of Titus using the tools you've just learned so that you can see what God's word has to say – for yourself!

I chose Titus for a few reasons.

1. It's short. Just three chapters. This means you're less likely to be overwhelmed by too much detail.
2. It's written to an individual, not a group. As a figure in the Bible, we can see a lot about Titus. This helps with Audience Identification.
3. In this book, Paul is simple, direct and practical. I think this makes it easier to follow what he has to say.

All of this was carefully selected to help you have a great experience with this study.

We'll do this study together. This book will become your study workbook. I'll ask all the questions that go into the study and I've created spaces for you to write your answers. This will help make things simpler for you this time around. Later on, you'll be able to create your own format for collecting data. This time, work with me.

I'll also answer all the questions myself. This way you can have an opportunity to see how I approach the study. The goal is not for you to match my answers exactly. Rather, this will offer you another perspective on how the questions could be answered.

I encourage you to do the study for yourself before reading my answers. Remember, this is about you learning how to do this for yourself, not getting "the right answer".

It will probably feel a little strange doing this the first time. That's how every new skill feels when you start out. It's not really strange or hard. It's just new. When you've done it a couple times, it won't be new any longer, and you'll become much more comfortable with the process.

Getting Started

We'll want to prepare our materials before we get too far into this process. One of the keys to success is having the right tools at the right time. Let's get that done now.

First, get a copy of the text of the book of Titus. I generally go to one of the websites I listed in chapter six and copy and paste the text into a Microsoft Word document. This way I have control of the formatting and output. I encourage you to do the same right now.

Leave the chapters and verse markers in. That's important for doing research (every other reference will talk about chapter and verse). I also suggest double spacing and at least 1.5 inches of margin. This will give ample room for jotting down notes and questions later.

If you're a list person, check this task as done! It's not a big or a hard thing, but it's a start and now you're on your way!

☐ *Print a copy of the text*

Think about how you want to mark up your text. I like colored pencils. But I also use regular pencils and sometimes I even use pens. You'll be starting out with markings, so this is an early, not a late, decision. If you want to start simple, just use a pen or pencil.

Fair warning: there is a lot of writing ahead. If you don't mind writing in your book, you're set. But if you like to keep your book clean, then I encourage you to download the Study Guide and use it to complete your study of Titus.

You can download the Study Guide at:

https://www.dennis-stevenson.com/StudyGuide

As a reminder, here are the six steps we are going to follow:

1. **Read the text:** Establish the author, audience, and context
2. **Read the text**: Identify the author's message
3. **Identify questions that you want to answer**: Use your resources to find answers.
4. **Read the text**: Identify the author's message
5. **Map the audience & message**: Apply the message to your life
6. **Compare your conclusions with others**: Use any differences to expand your understanding

I've broken the book into four study sessions. This first session focuses on getting an overview of the book. Our goal is to get familiar with the text as a whole. To this end, in session one, we'll focus primarily on step one and step two. The final result will be a summary or overview of the book.

Many people struggle with summarization. They get caught up trying to be too precise. That's not necessary. Summarization is about hitting the high points and not getting distracted by all the little details. Once again, we're not searching for the perfect summary – just an ability to express the key ideas or key points.

I like to approach summarization by thinking about a few keywords I would use to communicate the big idea(s) to someone who hadn't read the passage. To them, it's all goodness. They haven't read the whole text, so they aren't in a position to judge me at all. All they can do is say "thank you." I think that's a good approach to summarization.

In sessions two through four we'll come back and focus on each of the chapters. Those sessions will focus largely on steps three through six. In those sessions, our goal is to go deep and see how much we can discover about what God has to say. With a smaller section, it will be easier to dig in.

Author Summary

To start off, we'll look at the author. Read through the entire book of Titus (all three chapters) and highlight or mark everything the author says about himself.

Summarize all the things you identified about the author here:

1. _____

2. _____

3. _____

4. _____

5. _____

6. _____

7. _____

8. _____

Don't worry if you didn't fill out all ten items. I didn't when I did the study. But you'd be surprised what you can glean out of careful observation. This is probably one of the biggest lessons you'll learn. Keeping your eyes open and practicing observation will yield far more benefit than you expect.

Audience Summary

The next step is to look at the audience. We can't interview them directly, but through the words of the text, we can learn a lot about them. We see how they relate to the message that is being provided. We can also infer a lot from what is or isn't said to them.

The audience is critical to us as we begin to apply the message to our lives. The audience's similarity or differences with us today will have a tremendous impact on how we map the message.

Read through the entire text again and highlight or mark everything the author says about his audience. Use your observation skills to find as many as you can. Personally, I read the text and with my colored pencil, highlight literally every word that about the audience.

Summarize all the things you identified about the audience here:

1. _____

2. _____

3. _____

4. _____

5. _____

6. _____

7. _____

8. _____

9. _____

10. _____

Stop and reflect for a moment. Is that list more or less than you expected you'd discover about the audience? Most people at this point realize that they were able to get significantly more information from observation than they thought they could. It's an encouragement that studying the Bible is not too difficult.

Key Word Summary

Now we are going to shift gears a bit and focus more on the message. Sometimes authors will use one word, or a group of words, over and over again. This serves to either establish emphasis or links different sections together in a way that helps us understand.

Other times, an author might be writing an especially logical message and use words like "since" or "therefore" throughout the text. If there are a lot of connecting words like what we discussed in chapter four, then we need to be aware of them.

We're going to read the book one more time and look for words that jump out at us. That can be because they seem to be used everywhere, or because they are critical to the flow of the text. Highlight or mark these so you can see where they occur. Sometimes we gain additional insight from seeing the distribution of these words.

If you mark it out by hand, you can see where these words are concentrated, or even absent. This gives a good map of the book and how the message is being constructed. This will be useful later when we come back to the text in more detail.

———————————————

Summarize all the key words you discovered in the book:

1. _____

2. _____

3. _____

4. _____

5. _____

6. _____

———————————————

You can also write down general observations about the text and how it flows. Sometimes these observations lead to the best insights to the passage.

Paragraph Summary

Let's boil the entire book down to a few words. We're going to do this paragraph by paragraph. When we get the paragraphs summarized, we will have a pretty good summary of the entire book.

If you recall from chapter three, paragraphs have an internal structure. Each paragraph is about one idea. It has a subject sentence and then a variety of sentences supporting that idea. We're going to use this paragraph structure to help us summarize.

Here's a trick when it comes to summarization. Instead of spending a lot of time and effort looking for just the right word, identify the subject sentence and pull out the one or two keywords from that sentence. Then add one or two other words that were used in the paragraph and which seem to carry special importance. Write out these words and you have a summarization.

Summarize each paragraph in the book:

1:1-4 _____

1:5-9 _____

1:10-16 _____

2:1-10 _____

2:11-15 _____

3:1-11 _____

3:12-14 _____

3:15 _____

If you stop and think about it, that means that there are only eight ideas or subjects that are being communicated. Everything else in the book is in support of these eight ideas. For me, this makes the book feel much smaller, simpler, and understandable.

Of course, if you want to study a much larger book, you might not be able to get this on a single page. But for a short book like Titus, it's a very manageable list.

Questions and Research

As you read, you might have come across a number of different things you didn't understand. You might have questions about the timeline of the book, or the historical setting of the book. You might want to know more about Titus and his relationship with Paul.

Write out the questions you are asking about the book of Titus. Keep this list focused on book-wide themes. You'll have time later to dig into detailed questions.

1. _____

2. _____

3. _____

4. _____

5. _____

6. _____

7. _____

8. _____

9. _____

10. _____

Now's the time to turn to whatever resources you have available to see if you can answer the questions. I suggested Bible Dictionaries, Bible Handbooks and Study Bibles as valuable resources to help get answers.

Use the rest of this page for notes from your research.

_____

_____

_____

_____

_____

_____

_____

_____

_____

_____

_____

_____

_____

_____

_____

_____

_____

_____

If you don't have any resources like I suggested, you might want to find a friend who has a few books you can borrow. You might also want to find a pastor or a well educated Christian you trust discuss these questions.

Of course, you could always go out and start your own Bible study library! If you are interested in the ongoing study of the Bible, these resources will pay big dividends. I have a starter list on my website.

https://www.Dennis-Stevenson.com/StudyReferences

Summarize the Text

This leads us to the last item in this study session. Summarize what you currently understand the book of Titus to be about. Don't worry, this isn't your final word on the book. It's just a marker that shows what you learned in this session.

Shoot for a summary of the information you've captured above:

- Who is the Author?
- Who is the Audience?
- What words seem to be important?
- What was the author's reason for writing?
- What key points were made?

This item should be in your own words, although you are free to use the words of the book as much as you want.

Congratulations on finishing the first session!

You did great! Remember this isn't about how much you know or how theologically astute your observations were. That kind of result only comes with time and study.

Success here is all about doing it! You've started and that's a major accomplishment. Too many Christians go through life never starting this kind of study. No one can ever accuse you of being part of that crowd again!

Let's Share Answers!

Let's jump ahead to step six for a little while now and look at what I found when I did the study myself. Remember the goal here is not to judge yourself in comparison to me. The goal is to gain another perspective on the study process.

If my answers are really different than yours, that's ok. Take advantage of this opportunity to go back to the text and see if you can see the points that I found. If you can do this, you'll get double value out of your study investment.

There's a possibility that when you first read the questions above you understood them in a specific way. When you read my responses, you'll be able to see how I approached the questions and what I was trying to get out of them. This might help you gain a better or deeper understanding of the questions and of the process.

Bottom line, I'm just another Bible student on my own journey. Let's collaborate and get better!

Here's what I discovered about the Author:

- The apostle Paul is the author
- Paul identifies himself as a servant of God and an apostle of Jesus Christ
- Paul defines his activity as preaching what he has been entrusted – and this comes from a command of God our Savior
- Paul was with Titus in Crete, but left him there and gave him

instructions about what to do.

- Paul describes his own history as foolish, disobedient, led astray, a slave to passions, full of malice, envious and hateful.
- Paul plans to winter at Nicopolis and wants Titus to meet him there after Artemas or Tychicus comes to relieve him at Crete

How did you do? If you want to re-read the book again and see if you can pick up where I found some of the information about Paul. If you found something I didn't list, congratulations for having sharp eyes!

Here's what I discovered about the audience:

- The single recipient of this letter is Titus
- Titus is like a son to Paul in faith (implying Paul was influential in his conversion?)
- Titus's task was to bring order to the church on Crete and see to the appointing of proper elders/overseers in the various towns.
- Titus came from a similar ungodly background as Paul

I didn't find as much information about Titus as I did about Paul. That's ok. There's no rule that these lists have to be equal. But this is enough to get us started.

Notice that I even included a question about Paul's role in Titus' salvation? That's there because I wanted to be sure to remember to look deeper into that at a later time. It's ok to tag some of your observations with questions that trigger later research.

Now let's see what I found under my review of keywords:

- Commands (imperative sentences) are paired with explanations or reasons (that, since, so that, for, knowing). Even Paul's reference to the instructions he left Titus come with a reason (so that)
- Only once do commands stand alone with no explanation or reason – but these are looking back on a whole section where reasons are already given.

- Highlights two true or trustworthy statements
- And: extended to include "likewise" and some "or"
- But: Extended to include some "not"
- Seems to be a theme of manifested/appeared
- In matters not related to Titus's reason for being in Crete, Paul asks him to "do your best". It seems to be a different quality of instruction from the doctrinal instruction.
- The book seems to be a mixture of a few strong theology sections surrounded by very practical what-to-do sections.

You can see that here I not only included the keywords, but also some of my observations of the text and how it flows. That's also good to do because it helps create the patterns that the message will follow.

In my printed copy of the text, I used my colored pencils to highlight or circle some of the words that jumped out at me, either because of repetition or because they seemed like keywords.

- But, So that, For, Therefore, Since, And, Likewise (connecting words we discussed in chapter three)
- Teach/Train, Submissive, Obedient, Rebuke, These things (words or phrases that were repeated)

Because these words are marked on my copy of the text, they will jump out at me in later sessions when I start to dive deeper. By the time I'm done, my copy of the text is usually pretty well marked up.

The next step is to summarize each of the paragraphs. Here's what I came up with:

1:1-4	Paul: apostle for God's elect
1:5-9	Put in order!
1:10-16	Rebuke and silence deceivers!
2:1-10	Sound doctrine & good works
2:11-15	God's grace appeared
3:1-11	Devote to good works
3:12-14	Do your best
3:15	Greetings and farewell

Notice that these paragraph summaries don't necessarily make a very smooth flowing summary of the book. Rather each one is a key to understand the individual paragraph. At this point, we are just trying to get to the big ideas that are contained in the book.

I did have some questions about the book. They were mostly high-level context-oriented questions. But I wrote them down and used my resources to find some answers.

I'll list the questions here, and indicate which resource I used to find my answer. The answers I share here will be necessarily abbreviated from the reference materials. I'm just looking to provide a high-level overview.

When was this book written?

- [ESV Study Bible] Mid-60's AD; Between Paul's 1st and 2nd imprisonment in Rome. This is approximate only; there is no textual evidence; goes mostly on tradition.

What were the circumstances of Paul's visit to Crete?

- [Halley's Bible Handbook] Probably on his way east (toward Jerusalem) after being released from his first Roman imprisonment. This occurs after the narrative of Acts ends. Like the question of timing, it's approximate and not completely certain.
- [Unger's Bible Dictionary: Crete] Crete is an island in the Mediterranean. It is 150 miles long 6-35 miles wide. Paul stopped there in Fair Haven while a prisoner on his way to Rome the first time. Traditionally Titus ended up there as the bishop over all the churches on the island

What do we know of Titus's personal history?

- [Unger's Bible Dictionary: Titus] He was converted by Paul, was a gentile, but not circumcised (Gal 2:3-5). He appeared to be one of Paul's traveling companions or protégés (similar to Timothy). He also dealt with the troubled church in Corinth for Paul. He was with Paul when Paul was arrested the second time and went with him to Rome where he traveled to Dalmatia (2 Timothy 4:10)

Who made the poem about the Cretans being liars? Is it true?

- [Unger's Bible Dictionary] The classics abound with references to the untruthfulness of the Cretans. This was frequently applied to them and the phrase *kretizein* (to play the Cretan) was synonymous with "to play the liar".
- [Halley's Bible Handbook] The quote is attributed to the Cretan poet, prophet and religious (pagan pantheon) reformer Epimenides (6th-5th Century BC)

There is an almost unlimited number of questions that you could have asked. These are the few that I chose to pursue.

This leads us to the last step of summarizing the entire book into a few sentences.

> Paul is writing to Titus his protégé after leaving him on Crete encouraging him to bring order to the Cretan churches by installing elders and rebuking those who would tear down the church with bad teaching while himself living an exemplary life of godliness. Paul emphasizes the hope in God that changes and motivates Christians to pursue godliness and resist wicked living.

Remember, summarizing is a skill. It takes time and practice. If your summary doesn't look or sound like mine, don't lose heart. The real benefit of summarizing is not the final result, but the thought process that goes on in your head and heart to come up with the summary.

Congratulations! You did it!!

That does it for session one! Take a moment and review your answers and remember how this study process felt. This will get even better with time.

Every time you approach a new Bible study, the first session will follow this pattern. It's a recipe for establishing the context of the book and starting to gather the relevant details so that you can build understanding and application.

Looking Ahead

In the next chapter, we'll dive into the first of three chapters in Titus and start to dig out the message and apply it to our lives. In that chapter, I'll introduce the deep-dive pattern for studying the text.

Chapter Eight

Understanding Titus Chapter 1

W ELCOME TO SESSION TWO of our study of Titus. In the last session, we looked at the book as a whole. This time we're going to dive deep into Titus chapter one.

In writing to Titus, Paul had some things he wanted to communicate. We will uncover those messages and then apply them to ourselves. Through Paul's writing, God is speaking His truth to us today.

Before diving into the text, let's review where we are in the process:

1. **Read the text:** Establish the author, audience, and context
2. **Read the text:** Identify the author's message
3. **Identify questions that you want to answer:** Use your resources to find answers.
4. **Read the text:** Identify the author's message
5. **Map the audience & message:** Apply the message to your life
6. **Compare your conclusions with others:** Use any differences to expand your understanding

In this session, we are going to focus on steps two through five of the process. All of our attention will be placed on Titus chapter one; that's only sixteen verses. Our goal is to develop a good understanding of what Paul has to say in this piece of the text.

We've already looked at the context of the entire book. You can look back to chapter seven at your notes (or my notes) on the big picture.

To summarize, the apostle Paul has left his protégé and ministry partner Titus on the island of Crete. Clearly, things are in disorder there. Paul gives very clear instructions that Titus is supposed to put things back in order and appoint proper elders in all the churches. It also seems that there is a problem of people circulating false teachings. Titus is supposed to oppose and silence those who are leading the church astray and present sound doctrine. Paul takes a moment to reflect on what that looks like. Finally, Titus is to encourage the Christians on Crete to live godly lives and to model for them what that looks like.

You can see that this book is quite packed! Let's dive in and start exploring.

Identify the Message

The first step in the detailed study is to identify the message that the author (Paul) is communicating to the audience (Titus). Your best tool here is to read the chapter a few times. As you read, odds are, the message will start to come out.

You should be able to use all the notes and highlights from the previous session. This is one of the reasons why I encourage a printed copy - so you can leave notes and mark it up.

As you read the text again this time, feel free to make more notes. As I try to identify the message, I like to circle words and draw lines connecting parts of the text that are related. This helps me see how ideas are introduced, then developed.

Another thing I like to do is to focus in on the imperative sentences. These often form the backbone of a text. If the author wants the audience to do something, they will generally say so using the imperative structure. This is a good clue for the meaning of a text.

How should you identify the message? That's a great question, that doesn't have a single answer. You could focus on breaking the text down into an outline so you can see the sub-messages and how they relate to creating a greater message. You could focus on a summary sentence or two that represent all of the text. Or you could even come up with a series of statements that represent the key points of the author's message. The point is to do what works for you because there's not a right or wrong answer.

You may find that different texts work different ways and that over the course of a few chapters you'll end up using all of the above techniques. You might even come up with a few of your own.

Make notes on your copy of the text, then clean them up and summarize them below:

_____

_____

_____

_____

_____

_____

_____

_____

_____

_____

_____

_____

_____

Questions and Research

Once again we come to the topic of questions. After digging into the text, you've probably come up with some things you didn't know or understand. This is your chance to write them down and use your resources to find answers.

Let's start off with your questions. List them out here:

1. _____

2. _____

3. _____

4. _____

5. _____

6. _____

7. _____

8. _____

9. _____

10. _____

You don't have to have ten questions. Fill in as many as came to you. Once you have done so, you are free to start to use your resources to find answers. You can see how helpful these resources can be in terms of helping you understand what you are studying.

You may also find that you can't find answers to some questions. That's normal. This may be because you don't have the right resources, or perhaps you need more scholarly resources. It may also be that the questions you're answering don't have answers that we can look up.

If you can't find an answer, that's ok. It's always nice to get answers to every question, but there's no guarantee it will happen like that every time. Continue to write down the questions. Perhaps later you'll come across a resource that will help you answer the question.

Sometimes as Bible students, we have to work with ambiguity. There may be things we don't understand and can't get clarity on. This doesn't mean we're failing. It just means we don't know the answers to all the questions. Our job is to do the best we can with the information we have.

Use the section below to write out the results of your research:

_____

_____

_____

_____

_____

_____

_____

_____

_____

_____

_____

_____

_____

Refine the Message

Now that you've asked some questions and gotten some answers, take your new-found knowledge back to the text. Review what Paul is saying to Titus again and see if you have gained any further clarity.

Studying the Bible is an iterative process. Repetition is a key tool in your study plan. We use it liberally here in this approach. It's just not realistic to expect anyone to understand perfectly in one pass.

I encourage you to jot down your questions and answers in the margin of your text. You might need to abridge them somewhat to fit. That's ok. The goal is to put all the information where you can see it.

After you've reviewed the text and refined the message write out what you understand the message to be in the space below:

_____

_____

_____

_____

_____

_____

_____

_____

_____

_____

_____

Map the Audience

Now that you know what Paul is saying to Titus, it's time to begin applying God's word to your life. This begins by mapping the audience. The more we are like Titus, the more specifically the message applies. The less we are like Titus, the more general we have to become to apply it to ourselves.

In some instances, we might map a given audience multiple ways. This is especially true if they have different roles which relate to us differently. In the text for this session, we see Titus as a church leader, a believer and as a companion of Paul. Each one of these roles might map to us differently.

Take a moment and consider what you know about Titus from this session and last session and write out how it maps to us today:

_____

_____

_____

_____

_____

_____

For many Bible students, this is a very difficult task. However, I encourage you to go with your gut and trust the process and the Holy Spirit to guide you. You might not feel like you came to any profound conclusions. That's ok. Profound is not required here.

This is just one step in the overall study process. As you continue through the process, you might gain additional insight into the audience and how to map them. That's fine! Revise your mapping. There's no rule that says once you've done a step, you can't update it.

Map the Message to Apply to Yourself

Mapping the message is why we study the Bible. This is where we pause to listen to the voice of God in the text. Now that you've mapped the audience, it's time to apply that to the messages.

Remember, the closer the audience maps to us, the more directly the messages in the text apply to us. Conversely, the more remote the audience is from us, the more we have to identify the principles underlying the message and apply them to ourselves.

As you think about applying the message to yourself, consider these questions to identify the application-oriented aspects of the text:

- What commands must you obey?
- What truth must you hold dear?
- What error must you run away from?
- How is God revealed in the text?
- How is the gospel made clear?

Take your first attempt at mapping the message here:

_____

_____

_____

_____

_____

_____

_____

STUDY THE BIBLE - SIX EASY STEPS

Remember, you can see how I did it in the next section. But this will be most beneficial if you have gone through the process yourself. This is another of those skills where trust is essential, and practice is king.

Don't get too worried if it seems difficult now. This will change as you gain experience and practice. The main objective is to get in there and start doing it.

Make an Action Plan

This leads to the final question of the application process. It's not enough to simply know what to do. We need to put it into practice. The best way to do that is to develop specific plans and goals that require action in your life.

Ask yourself this question: What actions can I take in the next seven days that will demonstrate that what I wrote in the application is true?

If someone were observing your life, how would they see the application lived out? I'm not talking about a coworker who only sees you at work or a friend who only sees you on social occasions. I'm thinking about someone who was with you all the time and saw you in both your public and your private moments. How would that person know that you took the application seriously?

List out some specific things you could do to align with the truth in this text:

1. _____

2. _____

3. _____

4. _____

5. _____

If you remember all the way back to chapter one, this is why we read and study the Bible. We want to know what God has to say to us. We want to know how to live our lives in accordance with His instructions and commands.

As you go through this application process, that's exactly what you're doing. You're making the Bible completely personal. You're understanding how God is speaking through His word to you, in your circumstances, in your life.

It might not be as dramatic as an audible voice from heaven. It might not be something that has a lot of flamboyance. But, for centuries, this is the way the saints of God have understood how God wants them to live.

And now you're part of that assembly. You are studying God's word and applying it to your life! Congratulations on this dramatic accomplishment.

Let's Share Answers!

Once again I'll remind you that even though you've done this, it's a skill that takes time and practice. It's unlikely that you feel comfortable with the process. But that's the way every new skill starts.

It's really helpful to share your process with other believers on the journey. So I'll share my answers to chapter one with you. I hope this helps you gain perspective on how it can work, to give you more experience and more confidence in the process.

Remember (again) that my answers aren't better than yours. Even though I have more experience than you do, your answers are still important. I share mine here so you can see the different kinds of ways that the questions can be answered.

If you struggled with a particular question, that's fine. Look at how I answered it and think about the thought processes that could have led from the text (it's the same text) to the answer I provided. This is a valuable exercise for you as it will expand your experience and horizons of studying the Bible.

When it comes to identifying the message of a section of the text, I like to find out how all the ideas fit together. In some ways, I'm trying to imagine what the thought process was that led the author to write out the message in the way that they did.

To this end, I often use outlining as a tool to identify and organize all the different parts of a text. That's what I did in this case. I generated an outline of the chapter so I could see the overall flow of the text.

1. Salutation - Greetings
    a. From Paul, a servant of God and an apostle of Jesus Christ
        i. Teaching godliness to God's elect
        ii. Preaching hope to God's elect
            1. Based on God who does not lie
            2. Revealed by God
            3. Commanded by God
    b. To Titus my true child
        i. (do not stray from the authority you have from me)
2. Put what remained into order as I directed you
3. Appoint elders in every town as I directed you
    a. Qualifications of an overseer
        i. Musts
        ii. Must Not's
    b. The need for solid leadership (defend and protect the church)
        i. Overseers are God's stewards (agents)
        ii. Silence the deceivers
        iii. Rebuke the liars, evil beasts, and lazy gluttons to bring on sound faith
4. Theology point: Purity does not come from impurity
    a. Those who introduce corrupt teaching are defiled
    b. It does not matter what positives they bring to the table, everything that comes from them is defiled

      i.   What they look like: talking about God, but living for themselves and their lies

      ii.   By contrast, pure faith only comes from pure lives and pure doctrine

   c.   They are detestable, disobedient, unfit for any good work

From this outline, I can clearly see the four main points that jumped out at me. It's possible that point two and point three are related, but at this point in the study, I didn't really have a clear opinion about that.

As I observed in the overview session, Paul seems to cycle between practical instruction and theological explanation. This chapter is a clear example of that.

The salutation is reasonably theological, attributing Paul's authority and mission to the direct command of God. Paul also brings that authority into play when he calls Titus his "true child". That puts Paul in a position of authority over Titus like a parent has authority over their child.

The practical section relates to expanding on Paul's instructions to Titus to put the church in Crete in order and get appropriate elders or overseers into place. This is an important point, and Paul spends time explaining what a good elder looks like.

Finally, Paul wraps up this section explaining that those who teach false doctrines must be opposed and silenced. Paul goes on to make the theological point that corrupt teaching cannot produce godly living. This suggests that Titus should not accommodate or negotiate with these corrupt teachers, but rather remove them from the church entirely.

After looking at this section I did have some questions. I wrote them down and spent some time researching them in my resources.

Why does Paul open with such a formal, involved salutation when he is writing to Titus his protégé? The introduction is 70 words in Titus but only 51 combined in 1 & 2 Timothy + Philemon (the other 3 personal epistles).

- [ESV Study Bible] Only Romans and Galatians have longer introductions. Paul's salutation in Titus emphasizes /sets up the theological sections in 2:11-14 and 3:3-7.
- [Study] Offers a strong foundation grounding for Titus as Paul emphasizes what to do. Paul is emphasizing his divine commission and applying that authority to his commands to Titus.

What does Paul mean by "what remained" in v5? Had something happened to disrupt the church on Crete?

- The KJV translated "what remained" it as "the things that are wanting"
- I concluded that "remained" means "remained undone"
- This suggests the gospel had been preached and people had believed, but the work of building churches had not been completed

To whom is the rebuke in v13 directed?

- [Study] Seems to be directed toward the people who are introducing false teaching. This is the encroachment of compromise and error into the gospel that had been preached on Crete. This entire paragraph seems to be about the people on the island and the common leading astray

What does it mean to rebuke?

- [Interlinear] To refute leading to conviction on the part of the offender; has the overtone of bringing shame. Suggests that there is a response to the charges being brought. Carries the idea that the purpose is a change in the rebuked party, not just getting into an argument.

In this chapter, I used several new resources. Let me explain a little about them.

In the case of understanding the phrase "what remained", I chose to look at the verse in a different translation of the Bible in the hope that would offer a more clear translation. In the King James Bible, the phrase "the things that are wanting" helped me understand that this was talking about things that needed to be done, but hadn't yet been completed. Other translations can be useful tools to help clarify words that aren't clear.

In a couple of the questions, I didn't have access to resources to answer the questions. Instead, I went back to the text and continued to read it over and over to see if the text would reveal any clues to the questions I was asking. In both cases, I eventually was able to use the text itself to answer my questions.

It doesn't always work out that more study will answer a question in the text, but it's always an option. I would encourage you to remain engaged with the text as it has much more to it than you likely will see in the first few passes. As you practice and develop your skills of observation, you will find that you see more and more in the text.

The alternative here is to ask a question that can't be answered. That's also OK and will be something you will undoubtedly experience from time to time. Remember, this isn't a competition. You don't have to do everything perfectly. No matter how much you study and learn, there will still be more that you don't know.

Finally, I used an interlinear Bible. This is a special study Bible that prints that original Greek or Hebrew text alongside the translated English text. Generally, these kinds of Bibles also have cross-referenced dictionaries that allow you to see the definition of the underlying Greek or Hebrew word which was translated into English. This is the tool I used to look up the meaning of the Greek word translated as "rebuke".

Based on these questions and some more ongoing study of the text of Titus chapter one, I was able to come to a more refined understanding of the message of the entire passage.

In this case, I moved away from an outline format to what I thought was more a reflection of how Paul thought about what he was writing. This is just my opinion of what Paul was thinking. But it does support all the text that we were reading.

Be Grounded: Teach godliness in the church; preach hope based on God's reliability, as revealed by God, as commanded by God.

The Charge: Complete the task of establishing the churches on the island of Crete.

The Solution: Install elders in every church. Overseers must be above reproach, able to teach sound doctrine and refute bad doctrine

The Problem: In Crete, there are many who would lead astray and upset the faithful. They must be rebuked and brought back to the truth so the church is sound in faith and doctrine.

Spiritual Point: Good doctrine and faith will never come from defiled unbelieving lives. Truth only comes from truth. Life only comes from life. Those who have not believed are defiled in minds and conscience; unfit, disobedient, detestable in their influence on the church.

You can see that this is a more polished understanding of the text. It is my summary of the entire chapter. It's in my own words and seeks to faithfully represent the key points of the entire text.

Take some time and review the entire chapter and see if you can identify where each of the main points of my summary came from. If you want, compare it to the outline I shared a few pages ago. If you look closely, you can still see the outline in the textual summary.

You may not be able to do something like this right away. Don't fret. That's not the goal here. I have a lot of practice doing this and you have very little. With time and experience, you'll be able to come up with summaries like this.

Now we come to mapping the audience. How is Titus like us and how is he different from us. This will establish the pattern for how directly this message will impact my life and your life.

Titus is a believer, living under the power of the gospel, pursuing the mission of the church:

- Theologically he is very close to me.

Titus is acting on Paul's instruction and apostolic authority and is in charge of setting up churches

- Vocationally he is distant from me, but the things he is charged to do (setting up a healthy church) have direct application to me and represent principles I must honor in my church.

This leads me to the final step: applying this text in my own life. Now that I understand my relationship to Titus, I have all the information I need to apply God's word to my own life. I'll start with Paul's message to Titus and map it into my own life.

What commands must I obey?

- While I do not speak for the church, as a believer I should still rebuke and oppose the insubordinate, empty talkers and deceivers (they must be silenced, rebuke them sharply)

What truth must I hold dear?

- God's truth can only come from a gospel redeemed life. All other sources of truth are defiled.

How is God revealed?

- The promise and guarantor of eternal life

How is the gospel made clear?

- Without the gospel, defiled is the only option. It is not possible, apart from having a gospel-changed life, to understand and teach true doctrine.

Big Idea: A healthy gospel flourishes in a healthy church

1. Church leaders are God's stewards and must teach sound doctrine
2. Deceptive teachers abound and must be silenced
3. Only the gospel produces proper faith.

I found it easy to use the list of questions to help draw out the application of this passage. Since Titus is a believer like me, all the points about the gospel and the "empty talkers" have a very close application to me. That made that part pretty easy.

Titus is also an apostle-appointed church leader and I am not. Therefore Paul's instructions to "finish what remained" and to "appoint elders" don't really apply directly to me. However, I can see that there is a principle of church organization and structure that underlies Paul's commands to Titus. This principle holds true in the church today. It is important that churches have proper leaders who are able to correctly teach true doctrine and refute those who teach false doctrine.

This is an example of how we would take a direct command and look for the underlying principle that holds true. As members of the church, we can now see the importance and value of proper spiritual leadership in the church. If we were leaders, this would be applied as standards for the leadership we provided (teaching and rebuking).

I chose to summarize the application into a single big idea that had a couple supporting points. I do this because my pastor uses this approach in every sermon, and I find it helpful for bringing clarity to a particular text.

You will notice that the big idea isn't something that appears directly in the text. Instead, it is the idea that supports all the commands and teaching that we see in the passage. The churches on Crete were not healthy, and the island was subject to all sorts of corrupted teaching that did not advance the gospel.

Paul's commands to Titus were designed to correct the unhealthy situation and bring health to the churches of Crete. The implication was that when proper leaders were in place and the false teachers had been removed, the churches would be healthy and the gospel would be advanced properly.

I think you can pretty easily see how the three points under the Big Idea relate to the text that we studied. Clearly, the role of a church leader (elder) cannot be underestimated in terms of building healthy churches. The deceptive teachers needed to be addressed, and Paul's theological point was that only lives redeemed by the gospel can produce godly living – which is the outward demonstration of a vital faith.

Finally, this led to some specific actions for me:

What actions can I take in the next 7 days that will demonstrate that what I said above is real?

1. Evaluate my life – Am I living the gospel? How am I dealing with defiling influences?
2. Pray for my church leaders who bear this burden
3. Where am I tempted to compromise instead of rebuke or resist?

These are the applications that jumped out at me. Given the gravity of the passage and urgent nature of Paul's commands, I really saw that the needed areas of action were in self-evaluation (leading to change where necessary), prayer and a heightened awareness of my tendency to compromise my standards rather than standing up for the gospel.

I hope this has given you some ideas to think about. Don't spend too long on it. The most important thing here is to get a sense for how this process works.

Looking Ahead

In the next chapter, we'll dive into the second chapter of Titus. I'm very excited for you. This chapter will be different because of how much you learned studying Titus chapter one. Each time you study the Bible, it will be a little bit easier and a little bit clearer.

Pat yourself on the back. It doesn't matter how you think you did in this study. You did the study! That's what really matters. You're well on your way to getting better at this process.

Chapter Nine

UNDERSTANDING TITUS CHAPTER 2

WELCOME TO YOUR SECOND JOURNEY into studying a text of the Bible! You have so much more experience this time compared to last time in Titus chapter 1. Not only did you go through the process yourself, you also got ideas from looking at my answers.

The first time you study something, it's an adventure. The second time is a joy because it's no longer a mystery. That's you now.

I'll bet you've got some ideas about how to do this that you didn't have last time. That's good! Every time you study the Bible for a while now this is going to happen. You'll be learning from your experience and getting ideas.

Just to remember the process, here are the steps we're going through:

1. **Read the text:** Establish the author, audience, and context
2. **Read the text:** Identify the author's message
3. **Identify questions that you want to answer:** Use your resources to find answers.
4. **Read the text:** Identify the author's message
5. **Map the audience & message:** Apply the message to your life
6. **Compare your conclusions with others:** Use any differences to expand your understanding

Step one has already been covered. We did that back in chapter seven. You still have your notes on the printed text document. So we don't need to do that again. You've also done the first half of step five – mapping the audience. We did that back in chapter eight. We'll review it every time, but it probably won't change a lot.

The farther you go into this study, the more you will build up knowledge that supports the study process. It actually gets easier the more you study in a given book.

Identify the Message

We'll need to do this every time we study. Read the fifteen verses of Titus chapter two and dig into the message Paul is writing to Titus.

Remember, this is your preliminary understanding of the message. Don't worry if it's not polished. You'll have time to get to that later.

Put notes on your copy of the text. Be as neat or messy as you want. Then when you're done digging, summarize them here:

_____

_____

_____

_____

_____

_____

_____

_____

_____

_____

_____

_____

_____

_____

_____

_____

_____

_____

_____

_____

_____

How do you know when you've dug enough for this step? There's not really a right or wrong way to determine this. I can offer some guidelines that might help you determine the right amount of study here.

1. Give yourself enough time. It's not a race. There are no points for getting done quickly. I like to spend about thirty minutes to an hour on this step – but that's where I've ended up for myself. You might find thirty minutes or less is quite fine. Just don't hurry.
2. When you run into a lot of questions, it might be time to stop and do some research. At some point, too many questions can limit how much you understand, so let them be your guide.
3. Keep going until you get something. The purpose here is to find out what God has to say. Often, in the course of studying, you

will encounter an "Aha!" moment when some or all of the pieces click into place. That can be a good time to wrap up this step and move on.

If you think there's more, you can alternate between digging in, using resources to answer questions, refining what you've discovered, then digging in some more. You can go through that cycle as many times as you like until you get to the point of understanding.

Questions and Research

As you studied Titus chapter two, what questions came up for you? List them out so you can use resources to find answers.

- _____

- _____

- _____

- _____

- _____

- _____

- _____

- _____

- _____

- _____

The more you identify questions and use your resources to research them, the more familiar and comfortable you'll become with those tools. This will, in turn, help you get more out of those resources and gain ever deeper insights into the message you are reading.

Jot down your research and the answers. Don't forget to note what resource you used. If you ever want to go back and dig in later, this will be a real time saver.

_____

_____

_____

_____

_____

_____

_____

_____

_____

_____

_____

_____

_____

_____

_____

_____

_____

_____

Refine the Message

Go back to the text again and look with fresh eyes. Now that at least some of your questions have been answered, do you see connections that you didn't notice before? Is there a word or a phrase that jumps out at you when it didn't the first time? These are the kinds of things you'll be looking for as you begin refining the message.

I love this part of the process because I make so many notes on my copy of the text. I love to circle or mark words and draw lines that illustrate the linkages and development of ideas. This part of the process is exciting because the truth begins to emerge.

Summarize your refined understanding of the message below:

_____

_____

_____

_____

_____

_____

_____

_____

_____

_____

_____

_____

_____

Map the Audience

We did this back in Titus chapter one. Go back and look at your notes from that session. Once you've done this once, the mapping tends not to change very much.

If a major new aspect of the audience is introduced, then you might need to think about expanding or updating your audience mapping to account for that. But in this case, there's not really much of a change.

Just to be consistent with the process, we'll write down the audience mapping for each study session. This is actually helpful because it helps us remember how the audience of the book is similar and dissimilar to ourselves. This is an important thing to remember as we move on to the next step of mapping the meanings.

Copy, summarize or write out your audience mapping below:

_____

_____

_____

_____

_____

_____

_____

It's actually possible that you'll gain new insight into the audience from your detailed study of the text for this session. If that's the case, make sure your insights are reflected above.

Map the Message

This leads us to the key step of mapping the message. Remember that in areas where Titus is similar to us, we can take the message just as Paul communicated it to him. However, in situations where Titus is different from us, we have to look for the principle behind what Paul was saying.

Here are some helpful questions to guide your thought as you map the message:

- What commands must I obey?
- What truth must I hold dear?
- What error must I flee?
- How is God revealed?
- How is the gospel made clear?

Write out your application below:

_____

_____

_____

_____

_____

_____

_____

_____

_____

_____

Make an Action Plan

Don't forget to action plan now. Action planning is taking the message that you just identified and translating it into specific, meaningful things that demonstrate the truth in your life.

You can think of your action plan in terms like this:

- Things to start doing that you aren't doing now.
- Things to stop doing which you are doing now.
- Things to change and do differently than you are doing now.

The main goal here is to see where you can better align the way you live your life with God's communicated message to you. Your action plan can be very simple or elaborate, internal or external, relational or individual.

The main thing is that you want to make it something you can actually see in your own life. If it doesn't result in a difference, it's not an action plan.

What actions can you take in the next seven days that will demonstrate that the applied message you wrote down is real in your life?

Let's Share Answers!

This is the kind of study where sharing is encouraged – so long as you do your own study first. I'll share what I discovered when I did the study and you can compare your results to mine.

Remember, this isn't a competition and the goal here is not to see if you did well or poorly. I'm sharing so that you can see another approach to addressing all the steps. You should be able to get some insight into the process by looking at how I approached or thought about the questions.

When I started my initial pass to review Titus chapter two, I got a very strong sense that Paul was building up to something. How did I know that? I think it's because, in the first paragraph, Paul repeatedly uses the words *like* and *and*. These are connecting words that serve similar functions. They indicate similarity in ideas. With so much that is being linked this way, I started to think this had to be going somewhere.

This idea was confirmed when I saw that in the same paragraph, Paul used *that* or *so that* three times. These words indicate a result or an outcome. This pointed out that Paul was linking ideas together and showing the result.

Lastly, the second paragraph begins with *for* which introduces a reason for something. That second paragraph (verses eleven through fourteen) also has a very theological or doctrinal tone. This contrasts with the very practical action lists that I saw in the first paragraph.

Very quickly, I came to think that Paul was outlining a tangible plan of action and the spiritual reason why that plan matters. Since everything was pointing at the spiritual reason in verses eleven through fourteen, I thought I would look at the chapter backward and start with the big point being made and then follow the logic of how Paul got there.

Theological Truth:

- God's grace has appeared and saved us (from God's wrath which is the penalty for sin) and changed everything about us

STUDY THE BIBLE - SIX EASY STEPS

- From ungodliness and worldly passions - to self-controlled, upright and godly

Spiritual Outcome:

- The word of God is not mocked by unbelievers
- Opponents of God's work may be put to shame and not prevail against the church
- In all things, the doctrine of God our Savior is made beautiful (adorned)

Practical Living

- How should older men behave?
- How should mature women behave?
- How should young women behave?
- How should young men behave?
- How should slaves behave?
- How should Titus as a church leader behave?

I also saw that the chapter opened up with a command to teach sound doctrine and ended with a command to exhort and rebuke with authority. This bookends the passage and ties back to Paul's original instructions to focus on finishing what was left undone.

Looking at it backward and identifying the components seemed good because when I played it forward, there was a kind of logic that made good sense to me. All the pieces seemed to fall into a nice flow.

Paul's logic in Titus 2:

- Live Godly Lives (Paul gives practical examples)
- So that the correct Spiritual Outcomes will occur (glory to God and the gospel)
- Thereby fulfilling the Theological Truth (you are being transformed to be pure and a possession of Jesus)

This seemed like a good starting understanding. But I did run into some questions along the way. So I stopped here to use my resources and see if I could get further clarity.

What is the Doctrine of God our Savior?

- [ESV Study Bible] This is a setup for verses 11-14 which explain the doctrine.
- Paul seems to say "God our Savior" and then refine it later to be "our great God and Savior Jesus Christ". See also 1:3/4, 2:10/13; 3:4/6

Who is the "us" in verse eight?

- I could not find any real explanation of this in my resources, but I suspect it relates to Titus and Paul – representing the apostolic authority of the church.

What kind of training is being described in verse twelve?

- [Interlinear] To train children; to be instructed or taught or learn.

I will admit that I do like using my interlinear. It offers some study Bible notes, but most importantly to me, it offers a side by side of Greek words with English and cross-references the Greek words with a dictionary. This is helpful to get a deeper sense what was being said behind the word.

In the same way, English words have subtle variations. If I used the word "father" in a sentence or the word "dad" in a sentence, most people would pick up that the word father carries a more formal connotation and dad more familiar or casual. In the original language (Greek in the New Testament), words had similar subtle meanings.

In the example that I looked up, the word in verse twelve in the ESV was "training". But I memorized these verses as a young man in the King James Version where the word was "teaching". That difference triggered me to want to know more about what the word really meant.

What I discovered was that the original Greek word meant to train as one would a child. So the meaning is to show someone who doesn't know something how to do it so that they can do it. Think about teaching a child to tie their shoelaces.

That was pretty much it for my questions.

So now we're back to looking at what message I saw in the passage in my second pass. I think it's similar to the initial meaning but has a little more depth and detail.

The first thing I refined related to verse one. It's one of the strong exhortations from Paul and begins with the word "but". I finally decided that it was more associated with Chapter 1. Since "but" is a contrast word, it made sense that Paul would contrast the empty talkers with a command to Titus to be the opposite and teach sound doctrine.

After deciding this about verse one, I focused the rest of my attention into looking at the meaning in verses two through fifteen.

> Titus must impress on everyone in the church the impact of the doctrine of the great God and Savior Jesus Christ – which is the gospel:
>
> When Jesus **appeared the first time** as the demonstration of God's grace…
>
> - He brought salvation from God's judgment and redeemed us from lives of lawlessness
> - Through this salvation and redemption, He is transforming the way we live (showing us how to live differently) so we will be purified, fit for His own possession and eager to do good works
>
> Now we are waiting expectantly for Him to **appear again** in all His glory.
>
> As we wait, we should live lives that:
>
> - Do not let unbelievers make light of (revile) the gospel (word of God)
> - Remove the opportunity for anyone to criticize and oppose the work of God
> - Exalt the gospel and make it beautiful (adorn it)

Paul outlines how all walks of life should live to demonstrate their transformed lives and reflect the gospel:

- Aged men – Sober, dignified, self-controlled, sound in faith & love, steadfast
- Aged women – the same + reverent, not slanderers, not drunken, teachers of the young women
- Young women – love & submit to their husbands, love their children, self-controlled, pure, kind, industrious
- Young men – The same + self-controlled
- Slaves – submissive to masters, pleasing, not argumentative, not stealing, showing good faith
- Titus himself as a leader – model good works, show integrity, dignity and sound speech.

Here again, I thought that the big point Paul really wanted to get across was about "the doctrine of God our Savior". That is, he wanted Titus to make sure that people understood the transformation that had happened as a result of God's grace in the gospel and lived in accordance with it.

Once again I led with the big point of the gospel and tried to link all the implications that Paul attached to it. Clearly, Paul's vision of being a Christian is much more than just "get saved then get on with your life." He wanted to make sure Titus, and through him, the believers on the island of Crete, understood the power of the gospel.

Mapping the audience in chapter 2 is very similar to chapter 1:

Titus is a believer, living under the power of the gospel, pursuing the mission of the church:

- Theologically he is very close to me.

Titus is acting on Paul's instruction and apostolic authority and is in charge of setting up churches

- Vocationally he is distant from me, but the things he is charged to do (setting up a healthy church) have direct application to me and represent principles I must honor.

The believers in the churches on Crete are also an audience.

- In this passage, I think I hear Paul speaking directly to them through Titus. They are very similar to me in that they have the same relationship to the Gospel as I do.

I added the last bullet point because I thought Paul was actually dictating to Titus the message that needed to be delivered to the believers on Crete. In this, Titus is less the audience and more the mouthpiece.

I think that believers today are similar theologically to the believers in the first century. While our cultures are different, spiritually we are very similar.

This cultural difference comes into play when Paul provides the list of activities that everyone should follow. Culturally today we don't have slaves and masters. Paul is not advocating for slavery as a cultural institution.

Paul merely acknowledges that slavery exists in the culture of Crete. His exhortation or command is how the people who are slaves should behave. Specifically, he commands them to behave properly and honorably toward their masters. They are to be submissive to the authority of their masters, not argue with them, and not steal from them.

Paul's point here is that all the believers are to live lives which are pure for the sake of Jesus. There is no room for personal revenge, animosity or rebellion where Jesus has paid the entire price of sin. The same standard is applied to all of the people whose conduct Paul outlines.

This leads to the ultimate point of the study. Mapping the message to my life. Even in this passage, Paul is clear that the goal is to see real change in the lives that have been transformed by the gospel.

Here are the notes I wrote down:

What commands must I obey?

- Live in a way that brings honor and praise to the gospel and the Savior who paid for it. Many specific examples are detailed.

What truth must I hold dear?

- The gospel has saved me and changed me so that now I pursue purity and good works to be a fitting possession of Jesus Christ Himself.

What error must I flee?

- No error addressed in this chapter

How is God revealed?

- God is revealed through Jesus who has appeared in the flesh and will appear again in all the glory of God

How is the gospel made clear?

- The doctrine of God our Savior clearly lays out the entire gospel. Jesus appeared for the purpose of redeeming us. We who are redeemed should live transformed lives. Jesus is going to come again, and we wait eagerly for that.

What actions can I take in the next 7 days that will demonstrate what I said above is real?

- Reflection: In what areas is my life falling short of the purity befitting a possession of Jesus Christ? Make a list and pray daily for gospel power to begin to change those areas.

This passage makes great demands on us today. When we remember that our calling is to live pure lives that are suitable for Jesus to claim as His own possession, many of our small annoyances fade into the background. Yet how often do we let those issues take center stage?

Titus chapter two also points out to us our great need of the gospel's transforming power. On our own, we are not even close to capable to live the lives that Paul calls out. We need God's gospel power to be able to do that.

Paul's concern that we prevent others from mocking the gospel (verse five) or that we live lives that give no opportunity for criticism (verse eight) or that we make the gospel look beautiful (verse ten) ring true today. This is an element of the passage that is timeless.

The concern that Paul showed for the Cretan believers almost two thousand years ago holds true today. We are still waiting for Jesus to return. We still need to live lives that honor Him. Titus chapter two gives us a clear insight into what that looks like and how we should go about it.

Look at the list of lifestyle instructions in verses 2-10. They remain relevant today. They demonstrate a life that has been transformed by God. While they may be challenging (our humanity never likes to submit to anyone or anything), this is a vision of a mature Christian life.

Looking Ahead

In the next chapter, we'll dive into the final session in Titus. By now you should be starting to get a little bit of an idea of how this goes. I don't expect you to be perfect. It's probably too soon for that. But you are definitely gaining experience.

Dust off your pen and paper and get ready for a fun journey into God's word together. In the next session, you'll complete your first Bible book study! Can you believe it? I can. I knew you had it in you!!

Chapter Ten

UNDERSTANDING TITUS CHAPTER 3

C HAPTER THREE OF TITUS! This is the last one. You are about to complete your first complete study of the Bible. All you have to do is repeat the study process one more time.

Just to remember the process, here are the steps we're going through:

1. **Read the text:** Establish the author, audience, and context
2. **Read the text**: Identify the author's message
3. **Identify questions that you want to answer**: Use your resources to find answers.
4. **Read the text**: Identify the author's message
5. **Map the audience & message**: Apply the message to your life
6. **Compare your conclusions with others**: Use any differences to expand your understanding

By now that should start to feel familiar to you. That's the point. Practice and repetition lead to familiarity and comfort. If you keep doing this, you'll find that studying the Bible is easier and easier.

Without any further delay, let's get into the last fifteen verses of the book of Titus. It's time for Paul to wrap up his short letter to his friend and partner. He's not done with the important points yet, and he still needs to say goodbye.

Identify the Message

As you've seen from my answers in the previous couple sessions, the first version of the message isn't very polished or sophisticated. The goal is to start to identify the key message. Any way you can start to write that out is good.

There is always a temptation to want to be perfect. Often times, perfection is the enemy of an effective Bible study. I'm not saying that quality doesn't matter. I am saying that when perfection is the main goal, you've strayed from the objective.

As you work on the preliminary message this time don't worry so much about making it pretty or fancy. Just work to get the main points down. You're going to have an opportunity to come back later and polish it up.

Make notes on your copy of the text. There's no right or wrong way to do it. Then when you're done digging, summarize them here:

_____

_____

_____

_____

_____

_____

_____

_____

Questions and Research

What questions came up for you? Did you wonder who Artemas or Tychicus were? Did it cross your mind about the location of Nicopolis? Maybe you wanted to know more about the foolish controversies and genealogies.

That's great! Now's the time to use your resources to get those questions answered.

As you studied Titus chapter three, what questions came up for you? List them out so you can use resources to find answers.

- _____
- _____
- _____
- _____
- _____
- _____
- _____
- _____
- _____
- _____

Are you starting to get the idea that having questions is a good thing? It's not a sign that you're lacking, it's the vehicle for learning. Any time I sit down to study myself, I still find that I have questions that I want to know more about.

Use your resources to see if you can find answers. If you continually find that you ask questions that are outside of your resources, you can ask a trusted mature Christian for advice on more resources you could use to get more answers. This is a great way to discover new resources that are trustworthy.

Refine the Message

Now is your opportunity to re-engage the message and start to refine it. Hopefully, the research you did in the previous step brought fresh clarity to what Paul had to say. Go back to the text and spend some more time looking at what it has to say.

I often find that by focusing in on the keywords, I gain a lot of insight into the message. These connecting words help give me a real view of the way that the author is thinking and how they build from evidence to conclusion.

Summarize your refined understanding of the message below:

_____

_____

_____

_____

_____

_____

_____

_____

_____

_____

_____

_____

_____

Map the Audience

This is the third time in this study that we've gone through the process of mapping the audience. It's not necessary to find new aspects or dimensions of the audience to include in this review. It's fine if you look at the audience and realize that it's the same as a previous chapter.

The real value of this step now is reminding you of the audience and how they are like you or different than you. After spending time digging into the text, it's easy to forget who the audience is. The whole thing can start to feel very personal.

When we go back to mapping the audience, it's about re-grounding ourselves in the audience so we can apply the message correctly in our own lives. You may only spend five minutes reviewing your audience mapping notes. You may take a few more minutes to think about how the audience appears in this chapter. That's great. That's the point.

Map the Message

By mapping the audience, you are prepared to map the message. Where the audience is similar to you today, the message applies more directly. Where the audience is distant from you today, you'll need to find the principles behind the message to apply.

Finding the principles behind the message can be as easy as asking yourself "what is the truth that makes this message important?" Or you could focus on how the message points back to an attribute of God or the gospel.

Generally, when you are working with principles, once you've identified the principle, the next question is "what are you doing with it?" Are you living your life to show the principle is true? Or is there a part of your life that is out of step with the big principle? That's what you want to focus in on. That's the change in your life that this passage is pointed at.

Here are some helpful questions to guide your thought as you map the message:

- What commands must I obey?
- What truth must I hold dear?
- What error must I flee?
- How is God revealed?
- How is the gospel made clear?

Write out your application below:

_____

_____

_____

_____

_____

_____

_____

_____

Make an Action Plan

What are you prepared to do? If there is an area where you are short of what God wants, what are you prepared to do? If your life doesn't align with the message God is communicating, what are you going to do to remedy that?

The action plan is a key step to make sure that we don't stop at head knowledge about the Bible. It's not enough to know what is true. We need to live that truth in our lives every day.

Don't settle for the trap that tricks you into pointing at a point in your life when you were really out of line with the message. That was then. Let's focus on now. What part of your life today needs to be shifted? What thing do you need to do tomorrow to really embrace the message you've just uncovered?

Let's Share Answers!

I've studied Titus chapter three and I want to share with you what I came up with. I'm not saying that I'm right and you're wrong. I'll show you how I worked through all the steps so you can get a picture of how it can be done.

If there is a step where you don't like what you came up with, don't worry. Look at how I did it and see if you can find a better way to do it. Even better than that, go back and redo that step in your notes and see if it clarifies the rest of the study for you.

As I started looking at the chapter, I quickly saw that the tone of verse one seems to be a continuation of the end of Titus chapter two. Paul has some specific instructions for Titus and they flow together very well.

At the end of chapter two, Paul says "Declare these things…" At the beginning of chapter three, he says "Remind them…" This suggests a shift toward a retrospective message. First, Titus is commanded declare the truth and teach the people in the churches of Crete. Now Paul calls him to remind the people of the way that they should live.

In chapter three I also saw a small summary of the entire book up to this point. Paul has a specific message for the believers in the church. But he also has a specific message about those persons who have been stirring up and confusing the believers. Paul addresses both parties through his instructions to Titus.

As I read this passage, I could not shake the sense that the gospel was a primary theme that Paul wanted to address. He dives into a nice theological section in verses four through seven. This section seems to put the gospel at the center of his instructions about how to live and how to deal with the distractions that were causing the people to stumble in their faith.

The last big paragraph gives us some insight into the comings and goings at that time. But even in this very practical section, Paul manages to find a way to sneak in an object lesson on how good works can be taught.

In my first pass of looking at the message, I found my attention captivated by the gospel. It dominates my impressions and understandings of what Paul was trying to say.

Declare and Remind: Live holy, righteous lives

The Power of the Gospel

- It changed Paul & Titus' lives from rebellious to redeemed
- Even Paul & Titus needed the gospel to transform their lives. They were not above the gospel.

The Hope of the Gospel

- We are heirs and will receive an inheritance we do not deserve
- Because of the gospel, we look forward to something we did not earn on our own and could not achieve without God.

The Conduct of the Gospel

- Devoted to good works
- Paul lists out how people changed by the gospel ought to live their lives.

The Judgment of the Gospel

- Stay away from one who does not show the evidence of the gospel
- Paul is clear that those who do not demonstrate the gospel in their lives are not to be treated as brothers and sisters. They are to be set aside.

The Fruit of the Gospel

- You (Titus) care for the fellow ministers
- The people will care for each other
- Show the fruits of faith

Note: Paul employs a lot of contrast to make his points. The word *but* is used three times in the chapter. I think that's a lot for this contrast word.

Initially, I was pretty excited about how I could weave the gospel into all the points. It was premature. As you'll see later, the snappy outline did not last ongoing study.

I did have some questions about this chapter. Most of them focused on the paragraph that seemed to deal with all the personnel movement. I was really trying to understand if there was a deeper message to be understood.

What do we know of Artemas or Tychicus?

- [Unger's Bible Dictionary] Artemas is not mentioned anywhere else in the New Testament. We only know what we can infer from him here in this verse. Tradition holds that he was the bishop (lead pastor) in Lystra (a city in modern-day Turkey).
- [Unger's Bible Dictionary] Tychicus is referenced several times as being with Paul or working in conjunction with Paul. In Acts 20:4 he is called a native of Asia Minor. Tychicus went with Paul to Jerusalem after the third missionary journey and may have been present when Paul was arrested. Paul references him in several of his Epistles from prison (Colossians & Ephesians). Finally, it is possible that Tychicus had been with Titus during the collection of the offering for the impoverished Christians in Judea.
- That Paul is discussing the sending of so many of his co-workers around suggests that Paul was actively involved in the provision of leadership and direction to many fledgling churches around the Mediterranean.

What are Zenas the lawyer and Apollos doing?

- [Haley's Bible Handbook] The text does not really tell us anything about that. Apparently, they brought the letter to Titus, including the instruction that he was to provide them with whatever they needed.

Is there any significance to Nicopolis?

- [Unger's Bible Dictionary] No real significance. Several locations are possible, but the most likely seems to be on the Adriatic coast of Greece about one hundred miles from Corinth. It is possible that Nicopolis had good weather for spending a winter, leading to Paul's desire to go there.

The biggest insight I got from this question and answer process was to think about Paul sending so many young men around the region. Clearly, he had a lot to do or communicate. In a non-digital era, the only way he could exercise his leadership was to go in person or to send a representative. He had access to a team of disciples whom he trusted to deliver messages and provide leadership where needed.

Returning to the message of the passage, I tried to condense it. While I liked the way the gospel featured so prominently in the preliminary review, I thought it was too long. This leads me to the following meanings from Titus three.

Remember: Believers are to live transformed lives characterized by good works

- By the power of the Gospel (no one can do it on their own – even Paul & Titus required the gospel)
- Fueled by the hope of the Gospel (an inheritance of eternal life, not condemnation)
- Demonstrating the conduct of the Gospel (good works; excellent & profitable)

Avoid foolish entanglements and the people who promote them

- If they do not demonstrate the Gospel in their lives, have nothing more to do with them (they are unprofitable and worthless)

Do True Good Deeds (let the people learn)

- To give to those who are in urgent need
- Demonstrate fruit (not just lip service)

This message seems to fit better because Paul addresses what he wants for the believers on Crete in two sections, and divides them with instructions for the worthless, foolish people.

I continue to be struck by the central place given to the gospel in verses four through seven.

This leads us to map the audience. I did not see anything new in chapter three that would change my mapping from the previous chapters. So I just reiterated what I said in chapter one.

> Titus is a believer, living under the power of the gospel, pursuing the mission of the church:

- Theologically he is very close to me.

> Titus is acting on Paul's instruction and apostolic authority and is in charge of setting up churches

- Vocationally he is distant from me, but the things he is charged to do (teaching the believers how to live gospel transformed lives) have direct application to me and represent principles I must honor.

My application is mapped as very close to what Paul wrote to Titus. I see all of the discussion surrounding the gospel to be directly applicable to me. The exhortation to live a life characterized by good works is also directly applicable to me because, in this area, I am very close to Titus.

> What commands must I obey?

- Be submissive
- Be obedient
- Be ready for every good work
- Speak evil of no one
- Avoid quarreling
- Be gentle
- Be courteous toward all people
- Separate fellowship from those who do not live the gospel

What truth must I hold dear?

- I am saved because of the goodness of God, not myself
- I am an heir of God

What error must I flee?

- Avoid foolish controversies, genealogies, dissensions and quarrels about the law. These are not the gospel and do not have any power to change my life. They are distractions meant to lure me away from the power of God.

How is God revealed?

- God is revealed in the gospel that changes our lives

How is the gospel made clear?

- This passage features the gospel as the power that transforms our lives and gives us hope

What actions can I take in the next 7 days that will demonstrate what I said above is real?

- Pick a command that I'm not doing well and focus on obedience. This text is loaded with all sorts of direct commands that I should be following. What really struck me was how I talk about people at work. I want to do a better job of the command to "Speak evil of no one." I find it very easy to drop small snide remarks about others when they do not do what I want. This is an area in my life that requires gospel transformation.

Think through all the different commands in chapter three. It's quite a list! While it may be easy to pick just one to focus on, that's not the only goal. You may find that several commands need your attention.

The goal in writing out an application is not to find a way to make myself compliant. I'm not trying to justify my behavior or declare it "Christian". My goal is to look for ways that I can be even more profoundly marked by the gospel.

As you study, you will be tempted to skip over this part of the process. Resist. Remember all the way back to chapter one of this book where we considered how the Bible is the very words of God, preserved and delivered to us today. I don't want to treat God lightly when He communicates with me. I want to take it very much to heart.

That's what the application process is all about. Taking God's words to heart. There may be an occasional study where you don't find something really relevant to apply. But remember that we are studying for the purpose of greater obedience and holiness.

If you find yourself discounting the application, or frequently saying "nothing here applies to me" stop and take stock. Why are you studying the Bible in the first place? It's likely that your purpose has shifted on you, and it's no longer about hearing God's word and obeying but about getting the study done so you can say you did it.

This is a challenge that every student of the Bible must face. It takes intention and energy to inquire after what God has to say. If we relax our guard, that intention can shift. The first place we'll see it will be in the quality of our application.

Looking Back

We're at the end of this study, so we can't look ahead. Instead, take a moment and look back. Review the copy of the text that you have been working with. Look at the notes that you've written down there.

One of the great benefits of studying the Bible this way is that it leaves evidence behind. You now have a series of documents that contain the lessons and learning that you've gained throughout the study. All the work you've just gone through is now literally at your fingertips.

I like to take all the studies and put them in a binder. From time to time, I like to go back and look them over. It's really fun when I study a book of the Bible for a second or third time. I love to look at how my understanding shifts and changes. I also like to see how I applied it to the different studies.

I would encourage you to do the same. Get a binder or a folder and put your study in a safe place. Ideally, you'll be doing this again, and you'll create another set of study notes that will be helpful in your Christian journey.

This time you put a lot of your notes in this book. Next time, you won't have this book to write in. You'll be able to create more notes to pair with your copy of the text. I would recommend that you continue to follow the six steps and write out the answers to each one of the questions we've been considering. It will bring consistency to your study and help you hone your study skills.

That's it for this study. Keep reading because I do have some more things to share with you that you probably won't want to miss.

Chapter Eleven

WHAT NEXT?

YOU DID IT! You've studied an entire book in the Bible. I'll bet you had a bunch of doubts that you could do this when you started out. Now you know that you can do it.

This is a fantastic first step, but it's not the end of your journey. Now that you've done this once, it's important to follow it up with more repetition or practice. The truth is that if you don't practice regularly, the familiarity will fade and the skills will become rusty.

Don't get me wrong. I'm not saying that you have to study a book every week or even every month. But I do know, based on a lot of experience, that if you don't keep up with it, the skills will start to fade. That probably also means that your confidence will start to slide.

Fortunately, the solution is really easy!

You just need to set up a plan to practice a few more times so the skills can become ingrained. In the long term, studying the Bible is like riding a bicycle. Once you learn it well, it is relatively easy to pick it up again after some time off.

You have a couple options for ongoing practice. A really good one would be to check in at your local church and see if they have any

Bible studies going on. Often these studies meet on a weekly basis. You could very easily join one and continue to use the steps you learned in this book to practice the study.

Another option would be what I call a "study buddy". Find a friend who has similar goals to you and commit together to study the Bible. It would be ideal if your friend had also read this book and understood the same six steps that you're using. That would be a benefit to your shared study process. Then you could study together, encourage one another and compare notes together.

I want to offer you a third option. Since we just studied Titus together, I think it would be fun to do another book. I'm thinking it would be another relatively short book similar to Titus. Lately, I've been thinking about 1st Timothy.

I'm not going to write another book to do that. Instead, I'm creating a Study Team. This team will be people like you who want to build their skills of studying the Bible. Just like this book, it will let us study together and share what we find.

Join the Study Team

You can join the Study Team for free on my website. Just go to **www.Dennis-Stevenson.com/StudyTeam** and sign up with your name and email address. That's all the information I need.

I'll send you an email introducing the study, then about once per week after that, I'll follow up with an email that shares a study guide and my study results – just like we did here.

I also think I'm going to use the Study Team to share additional resources that I use. If you are looking for an opportunity to build your study library, this is a great way to get suggestions. You can even use them as birthday and Christmas gift suggestions to share with your family and friends.

As time goes on, I'll think of additional ways that we can study together. I'm sure I don't know everything yet. Ideas will come to me and I'll share them with you.

This is your cue to put down the book and sign up now. If you wait you might forget. I've got a page on my website just waiting to get you onto the Study Team.

www.Dennis-Stevenson.com/StudyTeam

I look forward to seeing you online!

One Last Thing

I really appreciate that you took the time to read this book all the way to the end! That's fantastic, and I hope you got a lot of value from this journey.

I believe deeply in what I've written here. It would mean a lot to me personally if you would go out to the retailer where you got this book and leave an honest review. This is a small thing you can do to partner with me and get the word out. Reviews tell other potential readers what to expect from the book. I would be honored if you would share your experience too.

If you enjoyed this book, you might also be interested in other books I've written.

DEVOTION – MEN IN THE BIBLE

Drawing from more than five years of leading Bible studies, this devotional book creates an authentic spiritual experience in a simple daily devotion. You might have a way you've always done devotions. This book will give you a fresh approach that will make the stories of men in the Bible come to life and speak directly to your life today. It also includes a guided devotional workbook you can use to journal thirty awesome Bible stories that are sure to touch you and leave you changed.

MEN IN THE BIBLE – SMALL GROUP STUDY GUIDE

Men in the Bible - Small Group Study Guide is an easy to read guide that will give you everything you need to get started and succeed.

- Three simple tools to amp up the dynamic of your men's small group.
- A new process that makes stories in the Bible come alive and feel like YOUR story.
- Step-by-Step instructions for organizing and running a small group

This unique approach opens the Bible in a surprising way that cuts through fear and uncertainty and opens men's hearts to the power of the Holy Spirit. If you are looking for an eight, twelve or sixteen-week program for men, this book contains everything you need.

Stay tuned. I plan to write more books in the future. Look for my books on the popular online storefronts!

I'd love to hear from you. You can find me on Facebook at AuthorDennisStevenson or Twitter at @AuthorDCSJr or visit my website at **https://www.Dennis-Stevenson.com**.

Epilogue

A MESSAGE FROM THE AUTHOR

W RITING THIS BOOK HAS BEEN A LONG JOURNEY I did not expect. Looking back over the process, it's been almost two and a half years since the idea of this book began to form. That's at least a full year longer than I had anticipated. I think the story of this book is worth telling. I hope it shows that what you've just read didn't all come in a flash of insight and wisdom. It took a lot of work and time.

As I said in the introduction, the core material began in a small group Bible study. This is true, but it's actually more toward the middle of the journey. A number of events had already happened to begin to create the idea of this book in my mind by that point.

In the fall of 2015, I was invited to a men's leadership training program. Pastor Adam Bailie, who wrote the Foreword, wanted to work with men who had a leadership influence across the church. The first topic for this program was how to study the Bible.

As I said in the introduction, most people don't know how to study the Bible because no one has showed them how. In the case of this group of men, that was partially true. Many of them had picked up a practical approach along the way, so I think everyone had some sort of idea how to study.

We used a fantastic book as our text for the class. J. Scott Duvall and J. Daniel Hayes are the authors of a popular seminary textbook on Bible study. It is 512 pages long. We didn't use that, but instead, we used their 160 page abridged paperback version.

While it was short, it was definitely giving us the best possible perspective and tools for how to study God's word. As we went through it chapter by chapter, I could see the shadows of how a much more comprehensive book could be constructed. I enjoyed it in that I felt like this was the real deal on studying the Bible.

As I watched some of the other men in this program, I noticed that they were struggling with the material. These weren't men who were immature or ignorant. Many of these men had been Christians for a long time and were well read on matters of theology and the Bible.

I began to think to myself that if the mature leaders of our church were going to find this challenging; the everyday Christian certainly would too. In the quiet part of my brain, I began to puzzle out how I would approach the topic of studying the Bible if I were going to teach to everyday Christians.

Not long after this, in the spring of 2016, my small group began our study of the book of Isaiah. We had a lot of people who were unfamiliar with the book and wanted to discover what it contained. So we began the program that I described in the introduction.

Isaiah is a tough book. It's not easy. Even our summary approach ended up being pretty confusing. Most confusing was how to engage with a text that just seemed strange and foreign. Isaiah isn't a narrative story or a letter with a purpose. It contains a bunch of independent pronouncements that don't always relate to each other.

We soldiered on through chapter thirty-nine, which is a natural break point in the flow of the book. That's when we decided to stop and see if we could get better prepared. By this point, it was the summer of 2016.

Of course, I now had almost six months of contemplation on how to introduce the idea of studying the Bible for everyday Christians. I jumped on the opportunity to try out my thoughts in this small group. I wanted to come up with an approach which would prepare everyday believers with the foundational skills so they could move on to more advanced tools without any difficulty.

I volunteered to lead a few weeks on how to study the Bible. I created the first version of this book, which was a series of outlines and worksheets that I handed out each week to guide our discussion.

We took 6 weeks, corresponding to chapters one through six, to learn the basic principles. We did what amounted to one chapter per week. After that, everyone felt much better. But we weren't done because I wanted to practice studying a simple book before we jumped back into Isaiah.

We spent four more weeks going through the book of Titus. We used exactly the same approach as chapters seven through ten. There were lots of questions about technique and how to use the tools. But we did them together. Doing the study was a great way to identify where questions still lurked and where people weren't clear.

When we resumed the Isaiah study, the difference was immediate and shocking! The people who were confused before suddenly stepped up their participation. Our discussions went to a whole new level. But most importantly, the entire small group felt like they "got it."

After the success of the resumed Isaiah study, I approached my pastor about teaching the same material as a class at church. I gave him my outline and small group handouts and he liked it. So began the second leg of this journey.

In order to have better materials for the class at church, I converted the entire program to a sixty-two page workbook. It blended explanation with questions and answers. I'm proud of it. I'd love to share it with you if you're interested. You can download it from my website at www.dennis-stevenson.com/studyworkbook. It's also grouped into six sections that match to the corresponding chapters in this book but it doesn't include the materials for the study of Titus.

By now this story is in the fall of 2016. I was ready to teach a weeknight class at the church. I thought this was the big goal, and I had completed the journey. Of course, I was completely mistaken.

No one registered or showed up. I spent the first evening of the study sitting in an empty room hoping that someone would show up. They didn't. I still have all the copies of the workbook stuck on a shelf in my office.

I didn't give up. I can at least say that much. God was gracious and got me through this tough situation. But it meant that the journey continued.

In the late spring or early summer of 2017, the discussion came up again about teaching a class. I leaped at the opportunity. Of course, by now, the workbook wasn't what I was thinking about. I wanted to have a full-blown book to support the class. I started writing the first six chapters in a rush of creativity.

But I couldn't finish it in time. I started writing in May and the class kicked off in November. I was still stuck somewhere in chapter four. I could come up with a lot of excuses, but that serves no benefit. Instead, I dusted off the workbook that I never used the previous year and used it as the material for the class.

I was very excited to teach this material again. It had been over a year since I first created it. It was fun, like going home to jump back into it.

The class wasn't large, but I could tell that those who attended were getting a lot out of it. This was exactly what I was looking for! I wanted people to gain the basic skills of studying the Bible.

When the class was over, one of the participants wrote me an email.

> I just had to tell you how appreciative I am for the class you taught. I am using the Better Bible Study handout to further help me understand what I read. It is making a tremendous difference! I'm so thankful I could cry.

I've kept the email. It's an encouragement to me that God uses material like this to change people's lives. I'm humbled to be a part of such a grand divine design.

On the heels of that class, I rededicated myself to this manuscript. It's the third time I've created the material. I think each time I've tried it's been more polished.

It wasn't easy. In January 2018 I picked up the half-finished manuscript again. It's been much more effort than I expected to get the manuscript to the point where I could write an "epilogue". I've worked late at night. I've worked early in the morning. I've missed television shows with my family. I've even taken vacation days from my job just so I could stay home and write.

The result is what you hold in your hands. To you, I hope it looks great and was useful. For me, it's been a journey of more than two and a half years and three different formats.

Thank you for reading this book. My prayer has always been to give people the skills to rightly handle God's word for themselves. I hope that you now have the confidence to pick up your Bible and study it.

Now go do it. Your study journey is just beginning. No one but God knows where it will take you. But the result, in the end, will be worthwhile. I'm confident of that.

God bless!

Dennis Stevenson
April 2018 – Chandler, AZ

Made in the USA
Monee, IL
27 April 2020